M000012705

GRUNGE SEATTLE

Justin Henderson

THE
History
PRESS

Published by The History Press
Charleston, SC
www.historypress.com

First published 2016
The History Press edition 2021

Manufactured in the United States

ISBN 9781467148856

Library of Congress Control Number: 2020948444

This content was originially published by Roaring Forties Press,
ISBN 9781938901546.

contents

acknowledgments

Thanks to Susan Silver, Art Chantry, Charles Peterson, Chris Hanzsek, Ed Fotheringham, Lisa Dutton, Pete Vogt, Karen Moskowitz, Michael Cozzi, Oscar Mraz, and all the others from whom I got the basic story. Thanks also to the writers of grunge books, especially Michael Azerrad and Clark Humphrey, and to the creators of websites on grunge, from whose work I borrowed much information and the odd quote. As always, this is for Donna and Jade.

downtown seattle

1. Experience Music Project/Science Fiction Museum and Hall of Fame: 325 5th Avenue N.
4. Metropolis: 207 2nd Avenue S.
5. Gorilla Gardens: 5th Avenue S. and S. Jackson Street
10. Terminal Sales Building: 1932 1st Avenue
11. Vogue: 2018 1st Avenue
12. Showbox: 1426 1st Avenue
15. Moore Theatre: 1932 2nd Avenue
16. OK Hotel: 212 Alaskan Way S.
17. Central Saloon: 207 1st Avenue S.
18. Off Ramp: 109 Eastlake Avenue E.
19. Motor Sports International Garage: Stewart Street and Yale Avenue N.
20. RKCNDY: 1812 Yale Avenue
21. Crocodile Café: 2200 2nd Avenue
22. Black Dog Forge: 2316 2nd Avenue
23. Cyclops Café: 2421 1st Avenue
25. Comet Tavern: 922 E. Pike Street
26. Neumos: 925 E. Pike Street
29. Seattle Center: 305 Harrison Street
30. Bad Animals Studio: 2212 4th Avenue

greater seattle

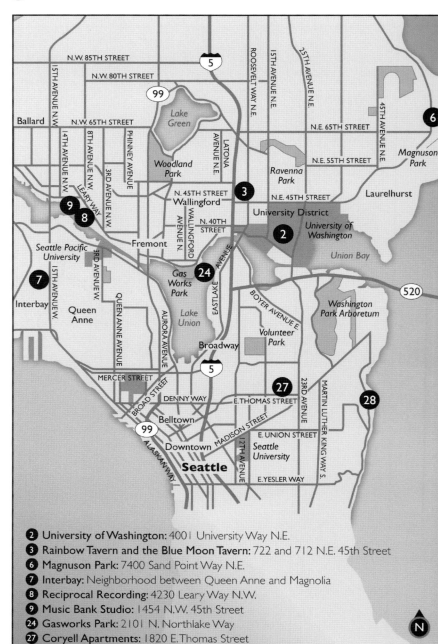

② University of Washington: 4001 University Way N.E.
③ Rainbow Tavern and the Blue Moon Tavern: 722 and 712 N.E. 45th Street
⑥ Magnuson Park: 7400 Sand Point Way N.E.
⑦ Interbay: Neighborhood between Queen Anne and Magnolia
⑧ Reciprocal Recording: 4230 Leary Way N.W.
⑨ Music Bank Studio: 1454 N.W. 45th Street
㉔ Gasworks Park: 2101 N. Northlake Way
㉗ Coryell Apartments: 1820 E. Thomas Street
㉘ Viretta Park: 151 Lake Washington Boulevard E.

the seattle region

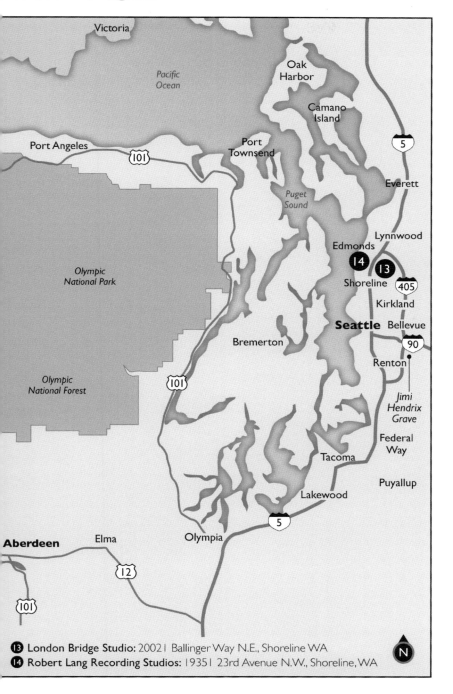

13 London Bridge Studio: 20021 Ballinger Way N.E., Shoreline WA
14 Robert Lang Recording Studios: 19351 23rd Avenue N.W., Shoreline, WA

GRUNGE SEATTLE

Seattle in 1990.

chapter 1

contemplating grunge

This book is intended to evoke a specific place—Seattle, Washington—during the era known as grunge, a rock-and-roll cultural explosion that occurred in Jet City in the years from the mid-1980s to the mid-1990s, as well as the grungy elements of the city as it exists today.

First, a quick reminder, since pop-culture memories tend to fade fast: before, during and after that ten-year period, countless bands in Seattle and elsewhere played music that passed for grunge, and we'll discuss a number of them in this book. But the four Northwest bands that eventually came to define grunge on the larger (more commercially successful) stage were Alice in Chains, Nirvana, Pearl Jam, and Soundgarden. These four bands, and a few other outfits, dominated the rock-and-roll world for a few years.

The roots of grunge can be found in the early to mid-1980s, and post-grunge aftershocks still ripple through the musical world today, years after the original Seattle grunge scene ended with a bang (goodbye, Kurt) and a whimper (when Soundgarden quietly disbanded). This book shows where grunge happened, taking a trip through Seattle and the surrounding territories, visiting the clubs, concert halls, recording studios, bars, coffee shops, streets, neighborhoods, and towns where grunge took root and grew from a close-knit community of like-minded and adventurous musical souls into a major international cultural—and commercial—juggernaut.

Speaking of commerce: Seattle is famous for originating a few things, and Microsoft, Boeing, Starbucks, Amazon, and grunge can arguably be considered the top five. Note that four of them are mega-corporations and one is a rock-and-roll movement. That is what makes grunge significant, in part: although Seattle has been home to important artists and major architects (and earlier moments of musical glory, it being the birthplace of both Jimi Hendrix and the song "Louie Louie"), the Rainy City's primary claims to fame have been its strikingly successful businesses, especially Boeing, Microsoft, and Amazon. These corporations have shaped the city into the vibrant regional capital and internationally known destination that it is today. For all its liberal cachet and green credentials, Seattle is and has always been mostly about money and business.

Because of this, and because it is relatively small, located at the edge—both literally and figuratively—of the cultural front, Seattle has often been a sort of also-ran, ruler of a region but a perennial runner-up in terms of national profile. This was true until grunge hit it big. And in the years since, though billionaire philanthropists have worked and spent assiduously to transform Seattle into a more culturally significant city, grunge remains the most influential cultural movement to arise in this city. As *Spin* magazine put it, in a story in December 1992, "Seattle is to the rock-and-roll world what Bethlehem was to Christianity."

Visually, too, the city has its icons and attractions: Pike Place Market, the Space Needle, the black monolith that is the Columbia Tower, the Seattle Public Library, various museums (especially the waterfront Olympic Sculpture Park), diverse distinctive and charming neighborhoods, surrounding evergreen forests, and the lakes and bodies of water that define and (dis)organize the city. And Mt. Rainier, majestically brooding in the distance. It's paradise, with perhaps a bit too much drizzly gray rain thrown in. All things considered, Seattle is a lovely place to inhabit or visit.

how seattle works

Let's take a more detailed look at the city and its surroundings, allowing those unfamiliar with Seattle to gain a sense of how it lays on the land and to figure out where some of the more interesting or unusual sites, monuments, and museums, grunge-related or otherwise, can be found on a map or on the street driving around. The words "driving around" are meant quite literally here, because like many automobile-addicted American cities, Seattle has a small and marginally effective mass transit system, consisting of a bus system and one light rail line—and yet Seattle is geographically complex. Although many of the grunge sites are reachable by bus (buses are free in the city center), many of the sites mentioned in this book are easier to visit by car.

Seattle is sheltered from the North Pacific to the west by the Olympic Peninsula, with the Olympic Mountains, and by the waters of Puget Sound, linked to the Pacific by the Strait of Juan de Fuca to the north of the city. Seattle is further sheltered by the (West Seattle) peninsula that curves around to enfold Elliott Bay. Seattle is temperate, with very few days of extreme hot or cold—but that seemingly ubiquitous, drizzly rain and the low dark northern sky that spits it out slowly and steadily for months at a time drives the city's residents to distraction. Distractions like grunge.

Seattle's many insular, close-knit neighborhoods are often defined, separated, or even isolated by hills or bodies of water. Capitol Hill, First Hill, Queen Anne Hill, Beacon Hill, Phinney Ridge, and other hills rise up, while Elliott Bay, Lake Union, Green Lake, the Ship Canal, the Ballard Locks, Portage Bay, Puget Sound, the Montlake Cut, and Lake Washington, which defines the eastern edge of the city, encircle and flow past.

East of Lake Washington is suburbia, ruled by Bellevue, and beyond Bellevue, the country and the mountains, blanketed by a once seemingly endless pine forest that has grown increasingly suburban in recent years. There are many bridges in Seattle, including several drawbridges that allow the passage of boats, infusing the city with a authentic maritime quality.

Major industrial activities take place close to residential area in Seattle, so you'll find grit in the gardens, working and middle-clas people in the bars and cafés along with crowds of yuppies, and th sound of freight trains slamming down the tracks along the waterfront blowing their long, haunting horns in the middle of the night. Tourist on the waterfront are occasionally confronted with the imposing sigh of a train blocking traffic, flatcars hauling the fuselages of Boeing air planes from Everett to Renton, or boxcars piled high with wheat from eastern Washington and lumber from the Cascades or Olympics. Ship bound for China wait in the hard-working harbor just south and wes of downtown, near the banks of the almost completely industrialize((and polluted) Duwamish River—where the native Americans lived and harvested salmon that fell like rain into their nets until 160-od(years ago.

New bike trails cross old railroad tracks. Luxury yachts compet(with fishing boats for mooring space in the waters of Interbay, wher(the fewer-in-number but still-busy boatmen of Seattle's once-thrivin; fishing industry are holed up, sneering at the yachties down the doc while patching their boats and waiting for the next crabbing or salmon fishing season to begin.

These offbeat interactions demonstrate, or at least suggest, tha in the last decades of the twentieth century, Seattle's economy was in ; period of transition (and occasional collision) between extractive anc constructive industry, on one hand, and information and service, or the other—and it still is. These days, much Seattle business takes plac(in cyberspace, and vast amounts of money sit in the bank account of myriad Seattle residents who've never seen the inside of a factory or a workshop. Yet Boeing still builds airplanes—or parts of them anyway—in the area, and factories still make real stuff here. Seattl(embraces and embodies a dynamic intermingling of nineteenth-, twen tieth-, and twenty-first-century economic energy. In other words, it i the perfect spot for a weird kind of rock-and-roll collision/dynami(

to take place, one that mingled punk, heavy metal, hard rock, sixties psychedelia, and dissonance.

Describing the lay of the land and identifying Seattle's natural and manmade icons is an easy trick. Identifying the places that carry the history of grunge in their bricks and boards and mortar is more difficult, for it presents Seattle in a more subtle way, in a different, dimmer light—call it the low light of inspired lowlife, for the grunge community emerged and made its statement, in large part, in basements, bars, performance halls, and nightclubs.

Much of what happened in the grunge era took place not only in downtown Seattle but also in satellite neighborhoods such as Belltown, Pioneer Square, Cascade, and Capitol Hill. These neighborhoods were and are close in, but in the 1980s they were slightly seedy—meaning cheap—and also, perhaps, slightly more inviting than other more settled areas: not entirely paved, not skyscrapered, not parking-garaged, not overwhelmed by concrete and metal, and thus a bit more accommodating to people who just wanted to hang out.

a point of view

Allow me to interject myself into the narrative for a moment. As a writer and a longtime rock-and-roll fan who moved to Seattle in 1991, at what was in retrospect the very peak of the grunge era, I was curious about the scene from the beginning. I came to Seattle from New York City, which along with LA formed the recognized bi-coastal center of America's musical universe. I had lived and partied through the late punk and new wave eras in New York. I had put in my time at CBGBs, hung out at Max's Kansas City toward its bitter end, and knew intimately the sooty, smoky, 3 a.m. shadows on the Mudd Club walls, the gender-free, sex- and cocaine-fueled bathrooms at Area, late nights at Mickey's, the Ritz, and other downtown clubs and bars. Burned out by a few too many early morning staggers home, I left New York in 1991, certain that my days on "the scene" were in the past, and that whatever came next would never compare to the glory days of Manhattan in the late 1970s and the 1980s, when Blondie the Ramones, Television, Patti Smith, the Cramps, the Talking Heads and two dozen other bands, all of them firmly planted in New York' increasingly mainstream underground, ruled the world.

In Seattle, I discovered a music scene that made up with pure mad energy and an unacknowledged but resilient community spirit what it lacked in so-called sophistication. I remember wondering at the time, how did this happen? I mean, come on, Seattle is a city, yes but it's a small town compared with New York or LA. How did this place manage to produce so many great rock-and-roll bands all at once within a few years? What was in the air, or was it the water? Was there an economic component to the sense of desperation expressed by many of the bands on the scene, or was it just oddball northwest juju?

Or was it a joke, a put-on that went ballistic, as half the bands up here proclaimed? In the documentary *Hype!*, the brilliant graphic designer Art Chantry, who cranked out hundreds of evocative, amusing, and visually compelling posters promoting concerts and club shows during the grunge years, said, "The northwest is where 'Louie Louie's from. . . . We have more unsolved serial killings here than any other place in the United States. I mean, the Manson family used to vacation up this way. This place is weird—a lot of occult stuff. All this stuff is a factor in what happened in the music."

Toss in soft, gray, unrelenting rain, add a shot of end-of-the continent isolation, stir in the countless other ingredients (most of them horny, pissed-off seventeen-year-olds) that make rock-and-roll re-invent itself every few years, and you have a moment. A movement That's how pop music emerged, time after time, before corporate mass media undertook to turn every single thing into a news story or a product, and that's what happened in Seattle. Grunge just . . . happened spontaneously, without rules or regulations or a guidebook on how to be grungy. And that, too, is one of the narratives about grunge—that the grunge scene in Seattle, before it hit internationally, was the last bastion of independent, regional rock-and-roll in America. The last time and place where a bunch of people could come together and make a lively, creative community happen without it being packaged and sold back by profiteers, cool hunters, and corporate drones dressed in hip drag, intent on finding the next new thing and figuring out how to sell it.

Grunge did become famous and commercial and full of itself, of course—but it took a while, and even after it happened, the scene continued on its merry way in Seattle. Some musicians got rich and some died, and some got rich and then died, while others chose to turn away from commercial success and just keep making uncompromising music—but whatever choices individuals and bands made, the music scene that took root in Seattle in the last two decades of the twentieth century remains vibrant today.

Post-grunge, or whatever you want to call this year's version of noisy, independent, small label rock-and-roll, is still in play. Seattle has changed drastically in the past few decades—some great, dingy bars and ramshackle nightclubs have disappeared under the wrecker's ball, replaced by ticky-tack condominiums with ground-floor franchise sandwich shops and pseudo-hip coffee bars all selling the same burnt black brew.

Who knows? There are still a lot of forgotten, quiet little towns around Washington and Oregon—and Idaho and Montana—and maybe in one of them, the new northwest music community is coming alive in next year's model of the teenage garage. However, with the rise of YouTube and the rest of the social (inter)network that holds us together and keeps us apart, the possibility that a quietly unfolding, uncorrupted new music community might develop unnoticed seems impossible today. Maybe it is true that in Seattle—ironically, since the computer world as we know it was born here, even if the Internet wasn't—grunge represented the last, valiant gasp of independent music in America.

Meanwhile, a look back at grunge gives us a chance to see how it happened, back in the last days of the web-free world.

To properly assess the grunge scene in Seattle, we need first to establish a historical and musical context. We'll begin with a short history of Seattle, and throw in a few musicians along the way.

seattle then:
the nineteenth century

The Duwamish tribe of Native Americans had a good run in what would later be called Seattle, a town named for a chief (Sealth) of the Duwamish and nearby Suquamish tribes—both of which were dispossessed by Europeans. By the 1850s, these tribes had been in the area for at least four thousand years. In 1851, when the white man first showed up, Native Americans inhabited a dozen or more villages along the banks of what would later be called the Duwamish River, where it met the sheltered waters of Puget Sound.

The white man arrived with the Denny Party, led by Arthur A. Denny. They settled first at Alki, in what is now West Seattle, and then moved to the more placid shores of Elliott Bay, near what is now downtown Seattle. Another party led by David Swinson "Doc" Maynard settled the land just to the south of the Denny stake. Soon thereafter, a man named Yesler opened the first steam-powered sawmill in the region, which began supplying logs and timber to San Francisco down the coast. Another settler, Charles Terry, sold his stake in Alki and moved to a spot just north of Maynard's. Later, Denny and Terry would hand over a chunk of land to establish the original campus of the University of Washington; Terry was instrumental in organizing the urban infrastructure of the growing city. Seattle was incorporated as a city in 1865, de-incorporated two years later due to "unrest," and re-incorporated two years after that. The town was rife with booze, prostitution, and gambling—most of it connected to Doc Maynard, according to legend.

A fitting tribute to Maynard, pioneer of the low life, can be found today in Pioneer Square, near downtown Seattle, longtime home to Doc Maynard's, a fine, grubby (grungy?) barroom that has been closed of late but may reopen soon. On the other hand, the lumber mill king Yesler—Seattle's first millionaire—is remembered by Yesler Way, formerly known as Skid Road (the term "Skid Row" derives from this), which terminated at the waterfront where his mill was located. According to legend, the logs skidded down the road to the mill, hence the name. Terry has streets named after him, as does Denny. But Denny is more famously remembered for the Denny Regrade, a section of Seattle just north of downtown that was once a hill but was regraded—that is, flattened—to create more level ground for development.

Seattle's early growth—and the formation of a strong labor movement—continued apace through the arrival of the railroad in 1884, the anti-Chinese rioting of 1885–86 (organized and led by labor union leaders), and up until 1889. On June 6 of that year, a fire burned most of the city to the ground. The city responded by passing new zoning laws requiring brick buildings, and a construction boom took off. The city quickly grew from 25,000 to 40,000 inhabitants, with the raunchy elements now loosely confined to south of Yesler's Skid Road mill. The city suffered along with the rest of the country from financial panics in 1893 and 1896.

In 1897, gold was discovered in the Klondike region of Canada, triggering the Klondike Gold Rush. Seattle established itself as the transportation and supply hub for the Alaska- and Canada-bound miners, and another boom ensued.

the twentieth century: the short version

The boom/bust mentality was and is par for the course in Seattle —and most everywhere else, really. It is the American way. The twentieth century witnessed a steady growth in the size and population of the city, as once-separate small towns and neighborhoods were an-nexed, year after year, and people were drawn to the city by assorted events—the Gold Rush; the Alaska-Yukon-Pacific Exposition of 1909; the growth of Boeing before, during, and after World War II; and the 1962 World's Fair, called the Century 21 Exposition (an Elvis movie was set there; today, the Seattle Center created around the World's Fair remains a large if slightly decrepit combination of green space, amuse-ment park, and urban gathering place not far from the heart of the city).

Racist though they may have been, the labor unions of the late nineteenth century laid the groundwork for what would be one of the most prolabor cities in the country—Seattle's General Strike of 1919 was the first such strike in the United States—and, perhaps, also cre-ated the socioeconomic dynamic that would eventually nurture the de-finitively liberal-minded, Democratic with a capital D city that Seattle is today.

A large blip in that steady upward growth curve occurred in the late 1960s and the 1970s, when Boeing suffered a major, if cyclical and predictable, downturn. Seattle's economy went south, and it felt like everybody left town. A couple of wise guy realtors even put up a billboard at the side of the freeway that read, "Will the last person leaving Seattle—turn out the lights." The population of Seattle actually fell, from 557,087 in 1960 to 493,846 in 1980, before the recovery of Boeing and the rise of Microsoft, Starbucks, and other native-grown Seattle corporations turned the city's economic fate around. There have been the usual ups and downs in the years since, but Seattle has been pretty much on a roll for the past few decades.

It is worth considering the rise of grunge in light of these economic patterns. This is a movement that took hold in the 1980s, when things were grim. Couple that with the usually dank, depress-ing weather and some interesting punky influences percolating in from overseas and up from down the coast, and you have the seeds of grunge. However, before getting grungy, we need to look more closely at a key component of Seattle's history—other kinds of music.

seattle's musical past

Not having witnessed grunge's early years, I can't speak from personal experience, but I feel compelled to wonder: Was there even one African-American on the grunge scene? Grunge may have been the whitest rock-and-roll movement in history. Yet Seattle's earlier musical history reveals important contributions from both Caucasians and African-Americans.

The jazz scene played a role in Seattle throughout the twentieth century, but its peak came between 1937 and 1951, with soldiers and bomber-building Boeing employees out looking for a good time in the form of live music and booze. There were a couple dozen jazz clubs on Jackson Street in the Central District in those years, and it was in these clubs that Quincy Jones, Ray Charles, and Ernestine Anderson, along with countless lesser-known others, got started. Many significant bands and musicians—W. C. Handy, Jelly Roll Morton, the Duke Ellington Orchestra, Lester Young, Charlie Parker—played gigs in Seattle before, during, and after that peak era. However, like most American cities in the first half of the twentieth century, Seattle was largely segregated, and these clubs were considered off-limit dens of iniquity by most of the mainstream press, the powers-that-be, and the cultural tastemakers. The mainstream missed out, it appears: Quincy Jones said, "Seattle in the 1940s was like New Orleans. Let the good times roll, 24/7."

In the early to mid-1960s, another little wavelet of a musical movement happened in Seattle and Tacoma, just down the road, with noisy, garage-style rock-and-roll played by a couple of bands, now semi-legendary, including the influential Sonics; the Ventures, who had a huge hit with "Walk Don't Run" in 1960; the Wailers (not Bob Marley's band from Jamaica), who put out a classic live album, *At the Castle*, in 1961; and the Kingsmen, whose once-controversial 1963 tune "Louie Louie," issued on Seattle's Jerden record label, surely ranks among the top ten most-played songs. (It is number five on *Rolling Stone*'s list of "Songs That Changed the World.") What other song can claim having an entire book—*Louie Louie: The History and Mythology of the World's Most Famous Rock-and-Roll Song*, by Dave Marsh—devoted to it?

Along with its one great song, this movement was significant, relevant to grunge and its more immediate predecessor, punk, in that these bands played loud and rough, especially the Sonics, who were noted for screaming and howling during songs, for customizing their amps to achieve fuzz tones, and for the twisted original songs they wrote and played along with the standards of the time. The Sonics' songs included "Psycho," "Strychnine," and "The Witch," three titles that could come right off a grunge album from thirty years later. Reunited after a twenty-five-year hiatus, the Sonics released an album in 2007; the Kingsmen toured in 2009 with two members from 1963 still in the band. "Louie Louie" lives!

No history of Seattle music can go without devoting attention to the one and only Jimi Hendrix, still considered by many to be the best player in the short history of the electric guitar (number one on *Rolling Stone's* 100 greatest guitarists of all time). Hendrix's career took off elsewhere, but he grew up in Seattle, played around a bit as a young man, wrote at least one song about a famous nightclub in the area, and inspired one of the city's most unusual museums, the Experience Music Project.

Jazz, garage bands, Jimi Hendrix, even the Beatles passed through, as did most of the other major and minor rock-and-roll stars and bands of the sixties and seventies. Aside from the unique place held by Hendrix, Seattle's musical history adds up to a fairly typical urban soundscape of twentieth-century America, one that was replicated, with regional and ethnic variations, in dozens of cities around the country. And then around 1980, the early stirrings of what came to be called grunge began to be heard in Seattle.

by the way #1

the experience music project/science fiction museum and hall of fame

Billionaire Paul Allen, a decent rock-and-roll guitarist himself, has been an avid collector of Jimi Hendrix memorabilia for years. Allen was never quite able to agree to terms with the Hendrix family, which rightfully controls his estate, and thus the ❶ **Experience Music Project/Science Fiction Museum and Hall of Fame** (325 5th Avenue N., www.empmuseum.org), which was originally intended as a kind of Hendrix museum expanded to include the whole world of rock-and-roll, does not include Hendrix's name in its own.

Designed by the wonderfully innovative architect Frank Gehry—seemingly to uphold the unfortunate maxim that "Seattle is where good architects do their bad buildings"— the strange, swooping, hulking building on the edge of the Seattle Center does have a lot of great rock-and-roll memorabilia, and anyone interested in the history of rock-and-roll in Seattle and the northwest should spend at least one day at the EMP. In an effort to enhance the museum's appeal, a science fiction museum was added to the mix inside the building, so pop culture fans can explore two major, fertile fields of interest in one visit.

by the way #2

jimi hendrix in seattle

Johnny Earl Hendrix was born in Seattle on November 27, 1942, and soon thereafter was renamed James Marshall Hendrix after a deceased uncle. He grew up in Seattle's Central District. Unusual for that era in segregated America, this was a mixed-race neighborhood. Years later, perhaps in part because of this, Hendrix would prove to be the ultimate crossover artist. During all-too-frequent periods of family turbulence, he lived with his grandmother in Vancouver, Washington, near the Oregon border. His parents divorced when he was nine, and his mother died in 1958.

Driven to perform at a young age, Hendrix as a kid first fake-played guitar on a broomstick, then played a one-string ukulele, graduating to an acoustic guitar at fourteen. His father bought him his first electric guitar at fifteen. He received his only failing grade in school that year—in music class! As a teenager, he played in a couple of local bands, and was known to be a big fan of both Elvis Presley, whom he saw perform live in 1957, and blues players such as Muddy Waters and B. B. King, whom he first heard on his father's records. He learned how to play a guitar with his teeth and behind his back, along with wild stage moves—an R&B tradition—from local performer Butch Snapes, who played guitar in a band called the Sharps.

History has it that Hendrix's first gig was with an unnamed band in the basement of a Central District synagogue—and that he got fired between sets for his antics on stage. He next joined the Velvetones, a local band that played regularly at a neighborhood gathering place called Yesler Terrace. Hendrix gained immediate notice for his trademark style of playing a right-handed guitar upside down, since he was left-handed.

Hendrix never quite graduated from Seattle's Garfield High School, although he was later recognized with an honorary diploma and a bust in the library. After a few low-level run-ins with the law, he ended up with a choice: go to jail or join the army. He joined the army and was discharged after one year—a good soldier he was not. Five or six years later—years spent in backup bands, on the road, hustling, learning, and jamming, playing the jobs and circuits available to an African-American guitarist in the early 1960s—Hendrix found himself in the right place at the right time—New York and then London at the birth of the hippie rock-and-roll moment—and emerged as the leader of the Jimi Hendrix Experience, one of the greatest rock bands of that first great rock era, the mid- to late 1960s.

What followed was a stunning, meteoric career, cut way too short. Hendrix's well-deserved legendary status as a guitar player—fueled by several brilliant albums and filmed performances at, among other renowned events, the Monterey Pop Festival and Woodstock—has only grown in the years since his untimely death, at 27, on September 18, 1970.

Hendrix's family still lives in the Seattle area, and a musical tourist in Seattle can visit several sites to connect with the Hendrix legacy. A statue of Hendrix playing guitar can be found near the intersection of Pine Street and Broadway on Capitol Hill in Seattle. The long-gone Spanish Castle Club, a mock-Moorish folly that rocked Seattle from its opening heyday in 1931 until well into the 1960s, is memorialized in the classic Hendrix tune "Spanish Castle Magic." The castle is gone, but the location on old Highway 99 between Tacoma and Seattle is well documented. His gravesite, a monument created by his family, can be found at the Greenwood Memorial Park in Renton, Washington. This is not the most thrilling site in the world—it doesn't have much soul, and a cemetery in a Puget Sound satellite city seems an odd place for this genius to end up—but it does hold Hendrix's remains, and is the final resting place for all the members of his family.

An early incarnation of Nirvana,
with (left to right) Krist Novoselic,
Kurt Cobain, and Chad Channing, who
would later be replaced by Dave Grohl.

chapter 2

pre-grunge grunge

Rock journalists, cultural critics, musical theorists, academics, bloggers, Wikipedians, and other scribes of varied stripes have obsessively documented the early years of grunge in Seattle in books and magazines and on the web. So it might be said that this book is beating its way down a well-worn path. Yet this is a different kind of book, and so the plan here is to pass through those early years with more of a focus on where things happened. We will cover the essentials of who-what-when-why, but the emphasis will be on where.

One part of the grunge story begins in the late 1970s, not in Washington but in Illinois, where three friends—Bruce Pavitt, Kim Thayil, and Hiro Yamamoto—decided after high school that they would move to Washington to attend college. Thayil and Yamamoto later would join forces with a drummer/singer from suburban Seattle named Chris Cornell and go on to found Soundgarden, but Pavitt first settled in Olympia, where he started a fanzine called *Subterranean Pop* around 1980. He soon shortened the name to *Sub Pop*, and began distributing compilation cassettes of underground rock bands along with issues of the magazine, both following in the footsteps of his fanzine forefathers and setting the stage for his later role as alternative music record company mogul.

Aside from serving as the location for Pavitt's first incarnation of Sub Pop, the capital city of Olympia, Washington, was not then and is not now a hotbed of cultural activity. Or maybe it's a minor hotbed. It is, after all, home to the progressive Evergreen State College, and it does have some alternative music cred, having spawned a loud and lively branch of the Riot Grrrls feminist rock-and-roll mini-movement. Several of the DJs running the college radio station, KAOS, in Olympia fiercely promoted independent, do-it-yourself rock-and-roll as well as the notion that the audience and the bands are equal, rather than the audience being worshippers crawling at the feet of their idols in the 1970s' rock-star mode. This egalitarian ideal percolated up I-5 to make its presence felt on the Seattle scene a few years later. Olympia also produced one great Northwest girl band (now in its second incarnation and considered better than ever), Sleater-Kinney (named for a road on the edge of town), and served as an incubator for Nirvana before they went on to conquer Seattle and take over the world. Olympia is not a city one needs to linger in, unless you're a lobbyist on a mission, but driving south from Seattle through Tacoma on I-5, once you pass Fort Lewis, you can view first the Sleater-Kinney Road off-ramp signs and then moments later the capitol dome as you zoom through Olympia on your way to Aberdeen, say, to pay homage to Kurt Cobain's seriously grungy small town roots.

mark arm: early grunge

But I digress. Bruce Pavitt moved up to Seattle and soon formed a partnership with Jonathan Poneman. The two of them subsequently transformed Pavitt's Sub Pop operation into the promotional monster-vehicle that drove grunge to the top of the charts. But in the early 1980s, before Sub Pop defined grunge, a couple of significant things were going on, though at the time, of course, nobody had a clue that they were in on the beginnings of a "scene" (everybody involved hated that term from the get-go) that would make rock-and-roll history a few years later.

Photographer Charles Peterson, whose black-and-white work in the 1980s and 1990s came to define the look of grunge, recalls that he first encountered this incipient Seattle music scene in a University of Washington dormitory around 1982, when he approached and started talking to another student, a guy wearing a Clash T-shirt. The guy turned out to be Mark Arm, formerly Mark McLaughlin, who would later emerge as the lead singer for Green River, considered by some to be the first grunge band; post-Green River, Arm started and sang lead in the seminal and long-lived grunge band Mudhoney. Peterson went on to make a name for himself as the primary photographic documentarian of grunge—his best work from that era can be seen in his book *Touch Me I'm Sick*, which borrowed its title from a classic Mudhoney song. The name Mudhoney, incidentally, comes from a 1960s film by trash-movie king Russ Meyer.

According to Clark Humphrey, author of *Loser: The Real Seattle Music Story*, the very first use of the word "grunge" in the context of Seattle music (the term derives from "grungy," a slang word first heard in the 1960s, meaning dirty or filthy) can be found in a letter Mark Arm wrote to Humphrey's fanzine, *Desperate Times*, in 1981. Arm, still using his given name, Mark McLaughlin, describes the music of his band, Mr. Epp and the Calculations—formed in 1980 and named for a math teacher at Bellevue Christian High School—as "Pure grunge! Pure noise! Pure shit!"

Arm, a devoted fan of new wave bands like Devo and seriously noisy punk bands like Flipper, was a local kid who surely ranks among the top ten characters in grunge history. Aside from possibly being the first person to use the word in a musical context and to have sung lead in one of the original grunge bands since the 1980s, Arm also knew both Sub Pop founders and has been friends with members of Soundgarden, Pearl Jam, and Alice in Chains for decades. Whether or not Arm gets personal credit for "inventing" grunge as a musical genre, he was present at the creation, since it was Green River that first achieved a (sort of) commercially viable version of what became known as grunge: a mix of Stooges-style punk, Black Sabbath metal, and arena rock à la

Aerosmith. Today, when not touring and recording with Mudhoney o doing side projects, Arm manages the warehouse at Sub Pop.

what is grunge?

Perhaps this is the moment to define grunge as a musical idiom As in, what is grunge? The two sources of influence cited in most grung narratives are musical and geographical. I would add a third, econom ics, and a fourth, attitude. And of course all these disparate influence are deeply interwoven.

First, the musical: Along with Seattle's own pre-grunge punk scene, exemplified by bands such as Ten Minute Warning, the Fartz the U-Men, the Fastbacks, and the Melvins, musical forebears included East Coast alternative bands such as Sonic Youth and the Pixies (Kur Cobain was a huge Pixies fan); pre-punk metal bands like Black Sabbath; Led Zeppelin; and hardcore, noise, and punk bands includ ing Black Flag and the Butthole Surfers from LA, and Flipper from San Francisco. Other influences are Iggy Pop and the Stooges, for th usual transgressive, stage-diving, self-mutilating reasons; British post punkers such as Gang of Four; and grand old rock-and-roll man Nei Young (he did some live shows with Pearl Jam) for the way he messed around with guitar feedback and distortion. There were others: ever grunge band in Seattle had its own set of influences, and each went it own way with those influences. For example, Nirvana used the Pixies soft verse, hard chorus construction in many of their songs, while Soundgarden often played arena-style rock like Led Zeppelin (while re jecting the macho sexism of arena rock bands) and mixed metal, punk and noise in the style of the Butthole Surfers. The one-label-fits-al grunge description came later, with the commercial success that fol lowed the creation of the "Seattle sound," as defined by the marketing wizards at Sub Pop.

The geographical inspiration behind grunge, though hard to imagine in the webbed world we live in, was one of isolation. A Sub Pop's Poneman once put it, "Seattle was a perfect example of secondary city with an active music scene that was completely ignored by an American media fixated on Los Angeles and New York." Mark Arm said, "This one corner of the map was being really inbred and ripping off each other's ideas." Producer Chris Hanzsek, who with Jack Endino ran Reciprocal Recording in Ballard for five years right through the heart of the grunge era, called it, simply, "a convergence of forces."

What you had were a bunch of bands playing for each other in the same venues, month after month, picking up the same influences, learning from each other, ripping each other off, ignored by the rest of the musical world even as they exploited what it had to offer them. And "ripping off" is not meant negatively here, since these guys were all pretty friendly—many of the players shifted around from band to band, forming and reforming in different configurations to shape a complex family tree of Seattle musicians. Notes photographer Peterson: "It was a small scene, and people all knew each other. People hooked up, and the scene grew organically." Producer Jack Endino, who recorded and mixed many of the most significant early grunge albums with Hanzsek and others at Reciprocal, recalled, "Nobody was too worried about success because . . . it wasn't LA. Nobody was going to come and sign us."

Then there was money, or more precisely the lack of (a need for) it. An important point to make regarding life in Seattle in the 1980s is simply that it was cheap! For a few hundred bucks a month, you could rent nice apartments or studios in one of the semibohemian enclaves around downtown, like Belltown or south Lake Union; even fine little bungalow houses in pleasant neighborhoods a little farther out (but still close in) could be had for what now seems like pocket change. A lot of these musicians who had to have "real" jobs to support themselves so they could play music didn't have to put their noses to the grindstone for too many hours a week. Art Chantry said, "People used to have these rent parties, where they'd hire a band, buy a keg, charge a few bucks, and make their next month's rent. The first time I saw Soundgarden play was at a rent party at this artist's house in Belltown." Imagine making your four-figure rent that way today!

Few artists live in Belltown these days unless they have been there so long their rents have become fossilized, paleontological relics of affordable, downscale Seattle. In the 1980s, Belltown was a pleasantly nondescript, slightly rundown little zone just north of downtown Seattle, dotted with weird little multiuse buildings, cafes, union halls, workshops, small apartment complexes, and assorted structures that could have been used for just about anything—and often were. Today, many of Belltown's streets are lined with massive condominium and apartment buildings and construction cranes, high-priced restaurants, pricey boutiques, and all the rest of what constitutes urman renewal in the twenty-first century. Although a shrinking number of nondescript little buildings still exist, housing hip stores, clubs, bar, and eateries, many of the funky old Belltown redoubts disappeared during the 1990s and 2000s, as American and international money flooded into Seattle and priced Bohemia out of town.

Finally, there is attitude—attitudes, really. The grunge stars who achieved major stardom and success as individuals and with their bands—Chris Cornell of Soundgarden, Eddie Vedder of Pearl Jam, Layne Staley with Alice in Chains, even Nirvana's Kurt Cobain, with his charmingly destructive, elfin energy—possessed that intangible star quality, charisma, at least when they were on stage. However, when you look at most of the grunge bands, what you see are a bunch of do-it-yourself regular joes, even nerds and geeks, some with charisma or talent, some entirely without. And whether they were stars or not, many of the musicians on the grunge scene shared a certain attitude: it was, says Lisa Dutton, a coproducer of *Hype!*, a "loser" mentality. What made it work was that it was shared by so many people, and it was as if they were all in on a huge joke—hey, we're rock-and-roll stars! But this joke was not always funny—and everybody knew it. Grunge was always recognized by its practitioners as half-serious and half a put-on, as many pointed out, but there is no doubt that the serious half reflected a real sense of alienation, anger, and disgust at American mass culture (and alienation from and disgust with the self as well). Consider these lines from Nirvana's "Smells Like Teen Spirit":

> I feel stupid and contagious
> here we are now entertain us
> a mulatto/an albino/a mosquito/my libido

(For those who don't remember, Teen Spirit was the name of an underarm deodorant for teenagers, back in the day.)

And then, through whatever combination of luck, talent, and timing, when a few of the bands hit the big time while most didn't, these feelings of anger and alienation—and the idea of it all being a big joke—got really confused. It becomes harder to laugh about rock stardom when your former roomie and bandmate, who quit your band to join another, is suddenly a millionaire rock star and you're still waiting tables. *Hype!* does a wonderful job of exploring these paradoxes of grunge success.

Rock-and-roll has always had its tragic side, and grunge did as well. Among those who did attain great commercial success were several who simply couldn't handle it at all. Some killed themselves, accidentally or otherwise. Others simply burned out. There's a reason Charles Peterson selected the title of the Mudhoney song, "Touch Me I'm Sick," for his book. It's a grunge anthem.

> Touch me I'm sick
> I feel bad and I've felt worse
> I'm a creep yeah I'm a jerk
> wow I won't live long and I'm full of rot

grunge in the u

Back to beginnings.

College dormitories, even those with historic grunge associations, are not tourist destinations, but the ❷ **University of Washington** (4001 University Way N.E.; www.washington.edu), where Peterson and Arm first met, is worth a visit. The Seattle campus is gorgeous, especially in springtime, when the cherry trees are in bloom, and its central quad is ringed by stately examples of neoclassical and neogothic architecture. The Suzzallo Library exemplifies this timeless institutional elegance, while the Henry Art Gallery on the campus edge blends old and new architectural styles in awkward yet challenging ways—and contains one of Seattle's most intriguing spaces for temporary exhibitions as well as a compelling permanent collection. Also on campus, the HUB Ballroom was the site of several legendary grunge shows, including an early, earth-shaking performance by Nirvana in 1989 in which the band displayed enough destructive energy to earn a permanent ban from the venue.

Nearby in the University District, visitors can discover a side-by-side slice of Seattle history with the ❸ **Rainbow Tavern and the Blue Moon Tavern** (722 and 712 N.E. 45th Street; Rainbow is closed, but the Blue Moon still has live bands nearly every night, bluemoon seattle.wordpress.com). Several major grunge bands played early-career shows at the Rainbow, including Green River and Soundgarden. Bruce Pavitt of Sub Pop booked shows there for a while, simultaneously reviewing rock shows for Seattle's semilegendary if rarely profitable alternative newspaper, the *Rocket*, building his indie cred, and making useful connections. The Blue Moon has a history not unlike the fabled White Horse Tavern in New York, complete with drunken poets, crazy beatniks, and mad professors. Saved in recent years from the wrecker's ball by the energy and passion of its own delirious denizens, past and present, the Blue Moon has been at the heart of Seattle's Bohemian culture since the 1930s.

downtown roots

For all that, the U was really not at the center of things in the pre-grunge days. The real show was beginning to take hold downtown, in a couple of bars in Pioneer Square and other random city dives. Possibly the most significant, or at least one of the earliest, of these new spots was the ❹ **Metropolis** (207 2nd Avenue S., in Pioneer Square; closed). The short-lived (1983–85) club served as a meeting ground and melting pot for musicians, actors, artists, and all sorts of oddballs and creative types. Susan Silver, manager of Alice in Chains and Soundgarden throughout the grunge era, more or less began her musical management career there, booking shows. She recalls it, fondly, as a place of community. "It was a cultural moment," she says. "The bands had been there all along—it was a strong community, but underground. It was a very community spirited and supportive scene."

Given the sort of alienated, antisocial vibe that many people associate with grunge (sensationalized drug overdoses, morbidly titled songs and albums, and suicides have fed that vibe), a sense of community is not something that immediately comes to mind. Yet in reading about the early years, talking to people, and viewing film from the time, that sense of community comes across as very real.

By the mid-1980s, a number of venues around Seattle accommodated the bands. Downtown Seattle was not a very lively place in those years—department stores were closing or fleeing to the 'burbs, the city was not yet on its high-tech roll, and many people were concerned that a dead city center was inevitable—but around its edges and in satellite neighborhoods there were a number of dingy yet spirited venues, including peculiar places such as the Odd Fellows Hall on Capitol Hill. More traditional were dives like the Ditto Tavern, the previously mentioned Rainbow Tavern, the Vogue on 1st Avenue, and the Central Saloon, one of the venerable Pioneer Square taverns that hosted grunge shows through the 1980s.

A joint called ❺ **Gorilla Gardens** (5th Avenue S. and S. Jackson Street; closed), on the edge of Seattle's International District (Chinatown), was one of the first places that booked both punk and metal bands, helping lead to a cessation of hostilities between two distinct music camps. The way Art Chantry tells it, the Gorilla started out as a Chinatown movie house divided down the middle, with a split-screen, split-theater setup. When it went from film to rock-and-roll, the promoter began booking punk shows on one side and metal shows on the other. "Now in those days," said Chantry, "the guys in these two musical camps hated each other, and many expected lobby riots as a matter of course. Instead, these disparate subcultures heard each others' sounds and liked them. In fact, aside from the haircuts they liked each other in general, the punks and the metal-heads." And thus, they merged and melded and mixed, and in the process invented grunge. Or one version of it, anyway. Another kind of moment in rock and-roll history was made at the Gorilla Gardens: with Seattle native Duff McKagan (formerly of Ten Minute Warning and the Fartz) on bass, rock-and-roll (anti)heroes Guns N' Roses played their very first show there.

the birth of soundgarden

By 1984, the stage was set for the next stage of grunge. Named for a sound-producing sculpture on the shore of Lake Washington in Seattle's **❻ Magnuson Park** (7400 Sand Point Way N.E.; the sculpture is still there, but these days "one only hears tones with strong breezes," www. seattle.gov/parks/magnuson/art.htm#noaa), Soundgarden was formed that year. Fronted by Chris Cornell and backed by Illinois college chums Kim Thayil and Hiro Yamamoto, the band opened for the U-Men in a show that September—and began performing at small venues around town, including the Rainbow Tavern in the University District and the Central Saloon in Pioneer Square.

Chris Cornell, who emerged as the star face and voice when Soundgarden later hit the big time, was born in 1964, and grew up with five siblings in middle-class Seattle, attending (and dropping out of) Shorewood High School. He worked as a seafood wholesaler and a sous chef (at Seattle's famed Ray's Boathouse restaurant) before starting his professional musical career. Cornell (born Christopher John Boyle—he and his siblings all took their mother's maiden name after his parents divorced) cites a two-year childhood stint listening to nothing but Beatles' records as his first inspiration as a songwriter and musician. On a more somber note, a year spent clinically depressed without leaving his house was the first of many such bouts Cornell has suffered throughout his life. He struggled with alcohol and drug abuse for years

When Soundgarden first started, Cornell played drums, but the quality of his voice (and his presence, no doubt—*Hype!* producer Lisa Dutton once called him "the most charismatic man I've ever met") soon led to the decision to put him out front and hire a drummer. The rest became rock-and-roll history.

green river at interbay

Possibly more significant than Soundgarden's formation was the startup of the band Green River, also launched in 1984. Named for a notorious serial killer from the region (the Green River Killer was finally captured, tried, and convicted of multiple murders some twenty years later), Green River consisted of several young veterans of the Seattle music scene, including Stone Gossard, Jeff Ament, Mark Arm, and Steve Turner. At one point during its short life as a band, Green River went into Chris Hanzsek's (and partner Tina Casale's) first studio, which abutted a rail-yard in ❼ **Interbay**, a gritty mixed-use industrial zone between Seattle's Queen Anne and Magnolia neighborhoods, and recorded a six-song EP for a label called Homestead Records. This recording, *Come on Down*, may have been the very first grunge record, although it remained unreleased until late in 1985. A disastrous cross-country tour coupled with conflicting musical interests sent Green River to an early demise, but two guys from the band, Mark Arm and Steve Turner, went on to form Mudhoney.

Interbay, where Hanzsek and Casale maintained their first studio, is a classic semi-grungy Seattle neighborhood—a marine-based industrial zone stuck between a pair of high-end residential enclaves, Magnolia and Queen Anne. Interbay is close to the waters of Elliott Bay, contains a huge rail-yard with multiple switching tracks, and abuts a busy boulevard. It houses dozens of boating and fishing industry wholesale and retail operations, acres of parking lots and disorganized postindustrial wasteland, and other visually or economically undesirable operations. However, times have changed somewhat: along with this industrial maritime zone, today Interbay is also home to a pitch-and-putt golf course and a P-Patch community garden. The area is being greedily eyeballed for redevelopment, and the opening of a Whole Foods supermarket sped things along. Being stuck between those two pricey residential neighborhoods—Queen Anne and Magnolia—tends to increase the chances that Interbay will soon be transformed into a sea of high-end condos, high-tech offices, and high-cost everything. But it hasn't happened just yet.

mingled roots

In 1985, a guy named Mark Lanegan and two brothers named Van and Gary Lee Conner found themselves to be the only fans of punk rock and psychedelia in Ellensburg, a pleasant, middle-sized Washington town located east of the Cascade Mountains, in farm country two or three hours by car and a thousand cultural light years from Seattle. They started a band in Ellensburg called Screaming Trees—you'd think forested Washington mountains and alienated teenagers got together to come up with that band name, but it is actually the name of a guitar distortion pedal—and after shifting a few people in and out of the band line-up, Screaming Trees cut a demo and landed a record contract, first with an outfit called Velvetone Records and then with SST, the punk record company. By 1988, the band had moved over the mountains and was firmly ensconced in the Seattle music scene, playing indie shows around the country, and working on side projects with everybody from Kurt Cobain to players from Tom Petty's Heartbreakers. Though they never made it really big commercially, various members of the Trees were highly influential players on the scene in Seattle and elsewhere for many years.

Many Seattleites insist that the very first grunge band was the Melvins, formed around 1980. With their Aberdeen connections, the Melvins were a major influence on Kurt Cobain; the point is, it doesn't really matter who was grungy first. There were dozens of bands, some local, some from other parts of the northwest or elsewhere in the United States. With partner Jack Endino, Chris Hanzsek ran ❽ **Reciprocal**

Recording (4230 Leary Way N.W.) in a dingy little triangular building between Fremont and Ballard (some call this nondescript neighborhood Freelard) from 1986 to 1991, and he says the studio was booked twelve to eighteen hours a day for months straight for most of those years. Their rates were cheap, they were in the city, they were open all the time, their ears were open to whatever people wanted to play—and there were countless bands on the move and on the make. He estimates that they recorded several hundred albums during that five-year run. (The building is still a recording studio but has had several different owners and names. For the past ten years or so, it has been home to the Hall of Justice Recording Studio, run by Chris Walla, formerly of Death Cab for Cutie.)

When grunge got big around 1990, some Seattle bands that had moved to LA to try to get record deals (people used to get paid, sometimes, to make records!) ended up moving back to Seattle to get on the Seattle sound gravy train. But they were interlopers. Mark Arm put it this way in an interview with Pitchfork Media. When asked, "Was there ever a band that said, 'Hey guys, let's start a grunge band,'" Arm said, "I'm sure there were. But by the time that sentence is said, you have missed the boat. You know what I mean? You're chasing a train that's left town."

Among the many 1980s, and early 1990s, Seattle performers and bands that didn't make it into this story but are more than deserving of mention are Tad, Skin Yard, Blood Circus, Gas Huffer, Dead Moon, Flop, Hammerbox, Love Battery, the Mono Men, Seaweed, Supersuckers, Pure Joy, Weather Theater, Still Falling, Swallow, the Fluid, Subvert, Coffin Break, Sadhappy, Pete Droge, War Babies, Metaphonics, Helltrout, the Fumes, Bitter End, the Thrown Ups, and the Young Fresh Fellows. Many of these bands, along with dozens of others not mentioned here, have sunk into obscurity, remembered only with the odd LP in a used record shop bin or stories here and there on the web—but some of the bands or band members are still around, playing regional, national, or international circuits, quietly proving what Pearl Jam more noisily and noticeably continues to prove: that what existed in Seattle in the 1980s and on into the mid-1990s was, indeed, what Susan Silver called a "cultural moment"—and it was a moment that had lasting power.

In our culture, such moments tend to attract people who want to package and sell them. And so it was with grunge: soon the big media and money arrived and things changed forever in musical Seattle—but let's save that "money changes everything" moment for later in the story.

nirvana's early incarnations

Down the road apiece, in Aberdeen, west of Olympia toward the Washington coast, at roughly the same time—1985—another seminal cultural event took place. Aberdeen is a rain-sodden harborside community that by the 1980s had fallen on hard times due to the near-collapse of its primary industry, logging. Around 1985, a couple of high school guys, marginally "troubled" youths named Kurt Cobain and Krist Novoselic, started playing music together. Enamored of all manner of weird-ass music, alternative rock, metal, punk, and everything in between, they were sensitive lads, semioutcasts (Cobain's parents had divorced in 1975, when he was eight years old) in Aberdeen, and so naturally they soon headed for a more accommodating cultural environment—the rock-and-roll scene in the nearest thing to Utopia— Olympia. From there it was but a short spin up I-5 to Seattle, once they got their act together. They went through a couple of drummers, tried out a few different names, and eventually settled on Dave Grohl, as the drummer, and on the name Nirvana.

deep six and reciprocal: the awakening

Early in 1986, Chris Hanzsek and his partner Tina Casale recorded an album called *Deep Six* on their own label, C/Z Records.

Released in March, the *Deep Six* collection of fourteen songs was the first C/Z Records album. More significantly, while *Come on Down* is considered by many to be the first grunge album, *Deep Six* got more attention. With each band getting four hours to record, the album included songs by Soundgarden, the Melvins, Malfunkshun, Skin Yard, Green River, and the U-Men. *Deep Six* unofficially originated the grunge aesthetic, although it would take the savvy guys at Sub Pop to formalize this aesthetic. Also in 1986, Bruce Pavitt of Sub Pop moved up from Olympia to Seattle and soon released an album called *Sub Pop 100*, a compilation of fourteen songs that also began to establish the Seattle sound.

In June 1986, Jack Endino and Chris Hanzsek took over Triangle Studios in Fremont and renamed it Reciprocal Recording. One of their first projects was another recording by Green River—a six-song EP called *Dry as a Bone*. Although the record wasn't released until July 1987, it has lasting significance for a couple of reasons. With Endino or Hanzsek at the dials, Reciprocal would become one of the scene's most important recording locales. And this was one of the very first records produced for Bruce Pavitt's Sub Pop label. A catalogue from the time describes this Green River EP as "ultraloose GRUNGE that destroyed the morals of a generation." There's the G word! The style of this record and subsequent Sub Pop products encompasses not only the sound of the music but the look of the packaging, with evocative if occasionally obscure black-and-white photography by Charles Peterson—often of the bands and their audiences at live shows—being the most obvious element in the package.

Later in 1986, Kim Thayil of Soundgarden introduced Pavitt to Jonathan Poneman; they became partners, turning Sub Pop into a real record label, and soon released the first Soundgarden EP, *Screaming Life*. During this period, Charles Peterson tirelessly shot many Seattle bands in concert at various venues, creating the sense that there was a big scene happening, when in reality these early grunge shows were often played for fewer than a dozen people, half of them members of other bands. But Poneman and Pavitt, who understood the dynamics of how music scenes can spring up in certain cities and regions, had come up with (or stumbled on to) the idea of creating an image that would somehow encompass the very different types of music being played in Seattle. Utilizing the style of recording and the look of the photos and the clothes—yes, musicians and their audiences often dressed similarly in ragged jeans or shorts over thermal leggings, flannel shirts, big boots or cheap sneakers, and watch caps—they began to create a buzz around grunge.

It is important to note that this wasn't entirely a question of packaging, promoting, and marketing. There really was something going on, a distinct and unique cultural moment. And flannel shirts really were commonplace in Seattle; because it is cold and damp, this basic, practical garb could be had cheap, especially secondhand at Value Village or Goodwill. Something was in the air that the Sub Pop guys were determined to bottle and sell. As music writer Michael Azerrad notes, while Seattle bands like Tad, Mudhoney, and Soundgarden sounded very different to their fans, "to the objective observer there were some distinct similarities."

Also in 1987, at the ❾ **Music Bank** (1454 N.W. 45th Street; closed) rehearsal studio in Seattle, a pair of struggling musicians named Layne Staley and Jerry Cantrell met and soon became friends, while living in the rehearsal space they rented. The band they formed went through a few names and incarnations, eventually settling on Alice in Chains (Staley had also an earlier band called Alice N' Chainz). They made a demo that in 1989 got them a record deal with Columbia. Within two years, they would be international rock-and-roll stars. It took that long because around about the time they finished the demo, the Music Bank got busted—in what was at the time the largest marijuana raid in the history of Washington state. But such setbacks failed to slow the momentum that was building. By the end of 1987, grunge was on the verge.

by the way #3

art chantry: grunge poster boy

Perhaps the single most influential nonmusician to have emerged from the grunge era in Seattle is a graphic designer, Art Chantry, who did more to define the look, feel, and even the attitude of grunge, visually speaking, than anyone else. In the years since grunge's peak (and during those peak years as well), Chantry has been recognized and honored worldwide for his brilliant, hilarious, and incisive graphic designs, not only for concert posters, but also for albums, plays, films, festivals, advertisements, and cultural pronouncements.

Chantry's a Tacoma kid, a northwestern native to the core, and so his take on the grunge scene and the weird northwest culture that spawned it is the real thing. He lived through it and was as much a part of it as any musician. You can see him in *Hype!*, destroying valuable samples of his own work while holding forth in his entertaining, opinionated fashion—he's surely the most articulate character in that very talky movie—and you can check out his work on numerous websites. He's won virtually every major international graphic design award; a monograph of his work has been published (*Some People Can't Surf*, by Julie Lasky); and his work has been exhibited in high (and low) art redoubts such as the Louvre, the Smithsonian, the Seattle Art Museum, PS 1 in New York (in association with the Museum of Modern Art), and, of course, the Rock-and-Roll Hall of Fame. For a dozen years, you could find his work on almost every telephone pole in Seattle, layer upon archaeological layer of club posters for gigs by a thousand different grunge bands. When the city banned pole postering (telephone repair people claimed they had difficulty climbing over the inches-thick layering of posters), another essential element of the grunge scene was laid to rest.

Chantry moved to Seattle after college up the road in Bellingham, couldn't find any corporate work, and ended up freelancing. Eventually, he landed at job at a new music magazine that started up in 1979, the *Rocket*, a now-legendary

Seattle rag where Chantry initially developed the look of grunge, what he termed a "roughed up" graphic style, while he worked as art director. The *Rocket* published from 1979 until 2000, and Chantry worked there on and off for ten years. During that time, he notes, "the magazine became a virtual hub on the wheel of Seattle's music and culture scene." Along with Chantry, *Rocket* alumni include Bruce Pavitt, who wrote music reviews before the Sub Pop record label took off; cartoonist Lynda Barry; cartoonist/TV impresario Matt Groening, creator of *The Simpsons*; writer Robert Ferrigno, first *Rocket* editor, later highly regarded thriller writer; and Charles Cross, editor for most of the newspaper's existence and author of several music-related books, including a Kurt Cobain biography.

Chantry's visual style—along with the talent he brings to the table—evolved in part as a response to low budgets and short deadlines. His work was/is about quick turnaround; appropriated materials; and playful, ironic, or just plain weird juxtapositions of different styles, messages, and signals. Whatever works. The low-tech, subversive, handmade look turned out to be perfect for the aesthetic of grunge, which was all about do-it-yourself and flipping the finger to the dictators of culture. But doing it yourself isn't worth squat if you don't do it well. Like the music of the best grunge bands, Chantry's work is unique—as roughed up or grungy as it might appear, it's visually compelling, amusing, thought-provoking, and utterly incisive when it comes to delivering whatever message is required, explicit or otherwise.

The first Sub Pop 200, released in December 1988, included three 12-inch
EPs with twenty songs from twenty bands, all but one from Washington state.
The bands included Soundgarden, Mudhoney, Green River, Blood Circus, Tad,
Screaming Trees, the Fastbacks, Swallow, and Nirvana.
The "Seattle sound," a.k.a. grunge, was about to conquer the world.

chapter 3

grunge's big moment

Toward the end of 1987, Green River broke up. The story about this breakup, at least in one popular version, points a self-righteous accusatory finger at Stone Gossard and Jeff Ament as being overly inclined to seek rock stardom by pursuing a more heavy metal style of playing, with whatever major label compromises that entailed, while purists Mark Arm and Steve Turner were committed to a punkier, less commercial sound, and with it, a more independent approach to music making, recording, and producing. Not in the least defensive about the issue, Ament later said that when he was in Green River he had a restaurant job to pay his rent, while everyone else got money from their parents. He said, "Did I want to play music and have my rent paid for? Hell yeah."

In retrospect, it seems that everybody got what they wanted. Arm and Turner found independence, respect, and even cult status with Mudhoney (who were and are loved in Seattle but are not nearly so well-known elsewhere). Ament and Gossard attained rock stardom with Pearl Jam, where they've been hanging out ever since. In any case, back in 1987, the breakup allowed Gossard and Ament to continue their work with former Malfunkshun singer Andrew Wood and band-mate Regan Hagar in the band they called Lords of the Wasteland. In December, the band recruited drummer Greg Gilmore to replace

Hagar. They began writing new material, and renamed themselves Mother Love Bone.

alice in chains arrives

As it turned out, in addition to being the year we elected the first George Bush, 1988 proved to be an important year in the grunge surge. In January, future Alice in Chains mates Layne Staley and Jerry Cantrell got serious about their work at the Music Bank studio; after going through several band names, including Diamond Lie (the one they used at their first gig), Mothra (after the Japanese sci-fi monster who duked it out with Godzilla in an epic C-movie), and even Fuck (not a good one for the record labels), they settled on Alice in Chains.

Layne Staley was born in the summer of 1967 in Kirkland, across Lake Washington from Seattle; his parents divorced when he was seven. This point is seemingly relevant since we have now three major grunge stars—Staley, Cobain, and Cornell—coming from broken homes. About his own parents' divorce, Staley said, "My world became a nightmare, there were just shadows around me. I got a call saying my dad had died, but my family always knew he was around doing all kinds of drugs. Since that call I always was wondering, 'Where is my dad?' I felt so sad for him and I missed him. He dropped out of my life for fifteen years." The connection to Staley's own fatal attraction to drugs cannot be missed or dismissed. Nor can the dark inspiration drugs provided, as is indicated by several Alice in Chains song titles: "God Smack," "Junkhead," "Hate to Feel."

Staley began playing drums at age twelve and played in various glam bands as a teenager, but he aspired to be a singer. As the story has it, his early band mates thought this a ridiculous notion—but Staley had the last laugh, emerging in the 1990s as one of the most intensely passionate vocalists of the grunge era.

Staley's partner in Alice, Jerry Cantrell, was born in Tacoma in 1966. His father fought in the Vietnam War—the Alice in Chains song "Rooster" was written by Cantrell for his father. A verse from the song illustrates how well Cantrell was able to evoke the Vietnam era, though he was still just a kid when the war ended:

> Gloria sent me pictures of my boy
> Got my pills 'gainst mosquito death
> My buddy's breathin' his dyin' breath
> Oh God please won't you help me make it through

"Rooster" was included on the album *Dirt,* released by Columbia Records in 1993.

Cantrell, whose mother was a pianist, started playing guitar as a teenager and played for years before meeting and becoming friends with Staley in 1987, when they formed Alice in Chains. By the end of Alice's first run, Cantrell was recognized as one of the greatest rock-and-roll guitar players of his era.

so does nirvana

On January 23, 1988, Nirvana materialized. Actually, they had already materialized. But this was the day they went into Jack Endino's Reciprocal Recording Studio to record their first demo.

Before looking at the results of this demo session, it might be useful to revisit the long and winding road up I-5 that Nirvana took to get from there—dingy downtown Aberdeen—to here—dingy Leary Avenue, west of Fremont and east of Ballard, in the depths of winter, January 1988.

Through the mid-1980s, Kurt Cobain was a stoned, scruffy, artistically inclined Aberdeen kid, from a broken home, living hand to mouth, trying a lot of drugs, edging his way into the music scene any way he could. Cobain's early life has been well documented, particularly in Michael Azerrad's *Come As You Are: The Story of Nirvana,* so there is no need to detail it here. The story in all its sordid glory is also told in Brett Morgen's documentary biography of Cobain, *Montage o,* *Heck*, released in 2015. But a short overview is in order.

Kurt was hanging around the Melvins in those days, going back and forth between Aberdeen, Olympia, and Seattle. He met Kris Novoselic around 1985, and also met his first significant girlfriend, Tracy Marander, at the Gorilla Gardens on an excursion to Seattle. Eventually he and Novoselic started playing together, practicing in various dives, basements, and an empty apartment above Novoselic's mother's beauty parlor in Aberdeen. By 1987, the two of them had gotten more or less serious about the band. They found a drummer—a guy named Aaron Burckhard. The party they were supposed to play for their first gig got busted, but they persevered and were hired to play another party, in the nearby town of Raymond. Nirvana's first live performance was a bust—they failed to make a splash at the party because they didn't play enough covers. Yet soon they were booked for a show at the GESCO Hall in Olympia. They drank a gallon of wine en route, played for ten people, and tore the place up. The next gig was at the Community World Theater in Tacoma. This was a converted porno theater, and a serious step up; bands like the Circle Jerks had played it. At this point, needing a name for the marquee, the as-yet-unnamed band called themselves Skid Row. In April 1987, they played a live show on the alt-rock Olympia radio station KAOS.

You might say they were on their way. Almost. In the next few months, they tried a few more names—Ted Ed Fred, Bliss, Throat Oyster, Pen Cap Chew, and Windowpane; Cobain at last landed on Nirvana, a Buddhist concept that means "the ineffable ultimate, in which one has attained disinterested wisdom." The Hindu definition describes it as "the transcendent state of freedom achieved by the extinction of desire and of individual consciousness." Cobain insisted that he "wanted a name that was kind of beautiful or nice or pretty instead of a mean, raunchy punk name like the Angry Samoans." And so the band became Nirvana, a name that Cobain later claimed he disliked. In any case, these guys were definitely not about the extinction of desire or individual consciousness. (Cobain later had to pay another band called Nirvana $50,000 to give up their rights to the name.)

Cobain lived a fairly reclusive life in Olympia, playing music with Novoselic and working dead-end jobs, but he was intent on pursuing the rock-and-roll life. Eventually, the two gave up on Burckhard, who did not want to leave Aberdeen and aspired to become a manager at Burger King. To keep the band going, they got Dale Crover from the Melvins to practice with them; after a few sessions, they decided to book some time at Reciprocal Recording in Fremont to make a demo. They went into the studio on January 23, 1988, and recorded ten songs with Jack Endino serving as engineer. He charged them for five, and Cobain paid the bill for $152.44 with money he'd made as a janitor. Novoselic had been laid off from his job, so he didn't have any cash.

Through Jack Endino's contacts, the demo got into the hands of Jonathan Poneman of Sub Pop, who said he was "thoroughly blown away by the guy's voice . . . I remember hearing that tape and going . . . oh my God!" Three of the songs from the demo—"Floyd the Barber," "Paper Cuts," and "Downer"—ended up on Nirvana's first album, *Bleach*, which Sub Pop released a year and a half later, in June 1989. But on that day in January, the foundation was laid for Nirvana's entry into the rock-and-roll pantheon. They played a show that night at the Community World Theater in Tacoma under the name Ted Ed Fred.

fremont and ballard

A few words on the Seattle neighborhoods near Reciprocal Recording are in order here. Reciprocal lies toward the Fremont end of Leary Way, a road between Ballard and Fremont that more or less parallels the Ship Canal connecting Lake Union to Puget Sound. Long known as the People's Republic of Fremont and acknowledged since the 1960s as the "center of the universe" and a stronghold of hippie, alternative, Bohemian, oddball, and hipster culture, Fremont has in recent years seen its funky streets beset by strains of the same virulent development that has so altered the rest of Seattle.

With hip corporations such as Adobe, Google, and Getty Images ensconced in office buildings edging Fremont, and new apartment buildings dominating the scene, Fremont ain't quite the same colorful place it once was. But the Fremont Troll is still there—an enormous concrete troll clutching a Volkswagen Beetle on N. 36th Street under the north end of the Aurora Bridge (check out fremont. com/about/fremonttroll-html/)—and Fremont's colorful and theatrical pranksters still put on an annual Summer Solstice Parade every year in June, complete with naked bikers, prancing fairies, fire eaters, stilt walkers, jugglers, dancers, clowns, and all manner of costumed, festooned, and dolled-up characters. Against the odds, Fremont struggles to remain a countercultural haven.

At the other end of Leary lies Ballard, Seattle's Scandinavian outpost. A separate town until 1906, it is the former shingle capital of the world, its old guard still yakking away with their "Yah sure" Scandinavian accents and scarfing up Norwegian delicacies such as the dreadful lutefisk between visits to the Nordic Heritage Museum. Ballard remains a vital hub of Seattle's maritime industry, although this industry is nothing like it was a few decades back.

On a rock-and-roll note, although in recent years condominium and apartment development has transformed Ballard into yet another outpost of upwardly mobile hipsters, Ballard's bar and pub scene remains lively, with spots such as the Tractor Tavern (www.tractortavern.com), the Sunset Tavern (www.sunsettavern.com), Hattie's Hat (www.hatties-hat.com), and the High Dive (www.highdiveseattle.com) in Fremont hanging on to their skanky roots and maintaining a high level of lowlife and good live music, ranging from alt-country semistars at the Tractor to local up-and-coming hard rock-and-roll at the High Dive. It's a different kind of buzz compared with 1988, but the good times do still roll.

mother love bone

As has been pointed out by several grunge scribes, most notably Kyle Anderson in *Accidental Revolution: The Story of Grunge*, what people talk about when they talk about grunge is a meeting of punk and metal; of arena rock in the mode of Aerosmith or Led Zeppelin, but somehow changed into something less . . . clichéd or obvious, yet still radio friendly. Still commercial. What they talk about, Anderson claims, sounds a lot like the music that was made by Mother Love Bone, the tragically short-lived band that Stone Gossard and Jeff Ament created with singer Andrew Wood and a couple of other musicians—Bruce Fairweather and Greg Gilmore—after Green River broke up. Mother Love Bone went into the Reciprocal Recording Studio in February 1988 to make their first demo—and it was obvious from the get-go that this band was bound for glory. They had the seeds of Pearl Jam's later greatness in the bass and guitar work of Ament and Gossard; they had flamboyant, audience-pleasing Andrew Wood out front; and they had a huge local fan base from their previous bands, Green River and Malfunkshun. During the band's brief tenure, Mother Love Bone ruled the Seattle music scene, and their live shows remain legendary.

Born in 1963 in Havre, Montana, Jeff Ament grew up Catholic and poor in Big Sandy, Montana, a town with a population of less than seven hundred where his father was mayor and drove a school bus. Ament began playing the bass guitar as a teenager, playing along with records by the Ramones, the Clash, and the Police. He was also a jock, playing basketball and football and running track at Big Sandy High School, from which he graduated in 1981. He went to the University of Montana to study art and play basketball, but dropped out in his sophomore year when the university discontinued its graphic design program. He moved to Seattle in the early 1980s with his band of the time, Deranged Diction. Eventually, he met Mark Arm and Steve Turner, and was asked to join their band, Green River, in 1984. Not long after, guitarist Stone Gossard joined the band as well.

Gossard was born in July 1966 in Seattle and grew up there along with his two sisters, Shelly and Star. His father was a successful attorney, and his mother worked in the city government. Gossard learned guitar while attending Seattle's Northwest School, from which he graduated in 1984.

Gossard's first band was called March of Crimes—another member of this band was Ben Shepherd, who later played bass in Soundgarden. Gossard became friends with the band's other guitarist, Steve Turner, and joined Turner in his band the Ducky Boys. Turner went on to form Green River with vocalist/guitarist Mark Arm, drummer Alex Vincent, and bassist Jeff Ament; soon thereafter, they asked Gossard to join the band. After the demise of Green River, Ament and Gossard formed Mother Love Bone.

sub pop scores

A few months later, in April 1988, Sub Pop Records, the fledgling record company, scored an infusion of cash and was able to hire some staffers, release more records, and move into penthouse offices in the ⑩ **Terminal Sales Building** (1932 1st Avenue). Mark Arm remembers: "They marked the beginning of the label on the day they moved into an office, so . . . people weren't just gathering at Bruce's house to stuff records, they were doing it in an office downtown. They moved in April 1988—that's why April Fool's Day is their birth date." That office would serve as the commercial heart of the grunge scene for years to come (and it was a serious den of iniquity, according to many who hung out there). (Sub Pop is now on the third floor of 2013 Fourth Avenue; www.subpop.com.)

nirvana plays the vogue

On April 24, 1988, Nirvana, with their new drummer Dave Foster (another kid from Aberdeen), played their first Seattle show.

They opened for a band called Blood Circus at the ⓫ **Vogue** (2018 1st Avenue; closed), a tiny nightclub on 1st Avenue less than a block north of the Terminal Sales Building. Seattle had few good rock-and-roll clubs at the time; the Vogue was nothing great. In previous incarnations, it had been a new wave club and a gay biker bar. The Vogue featured a transvestite bartender and was infused with the aroma of vanilla, which was actually the aroma of amyl nitrate—the floor was littered with emptied poppers of the drug used primarily in gay clubs to get a dance floor buzz on.

Over the years, the Vogue would host countless significant grunge performances, but according to most accounts of April 24, 1988, Nirvana's first-ever Seattle show wasn't one of them. Photographer Charles Peterson was there, and he was so unimpressed he didn't even bother to shoot photos of the band (another photographer, Rich Hansen, did take a few). Peterson, who eventually shot hundreds of great Nirvana photos, would later kick himself for that decision—such images would be worth a small fortune today. But at the time, with a few dozen people milling around and the mostly unknown Nirvana putting on a lackluster show, it didn't seem worthwhile.

The Vogue, and much of what defined grungy downtown Seattle in those days, has disappeared. In place of the Vogue is Vain, a hair salon popular with fashion-conscious Seattleites. Such changes were mostly for the better: in 1991, downtown Seattle verged on ghost town status—major stores were abandoning the retail core, there was only one movie theater, and the street corridors that linked the commercial center around 4th and 5th Avenues to the Pike Place Market overlooking the waterfront were besieged with hookers, drunks, and drug dealers. In the years since, Seattleites have witnessed the arrival of Pacific Place, a vertical shopping mall with a multiplex theater on top, another movie multiplex, a Gameworks arcade, a Cheesecake Factory, a Grand Hyatt and several other high-end hotels, a Nike store, posh bars, and all the rest of the somewhat obnoxious corporate, retail, restaurant, and commercial development that has brought downtown Seattle back to life and made it a place to go on a Saturday night. Hookers, drug dealers, and drunks still haunt the corridors connecting the core with the market, but there are fewer of them.

In spite of the corporate makeover, downtown still rocks. Pike Place Market (1501 Pike Place; www.pikeplacemarket.org; home of the original Starbucks) may be a tourist cliché, but so what? The market is still a cool place to walk, watch, and buy weird unnecessary stuff along with great fresh seafood, vegetables, artisanal cheeses, and breads, and the like. Buskers abound, and some are pretty good. Back in the grunge era, one named Artis the Spoonman was immortalized in a Soundgarden song, "Spoonman." He plays the spoons in the recording, and also in the video the band made for the song. The song lyrics, sampled here, were written by Chris Cornell:

> All my friends are brown and red, spoonman
> All my friends are skeletons
> They beat the rhythm with their bones
> Spoonman

The Seattle Art Museum is on 1st Avenue (1300 1st Avenue, www.seattleartmuseum.org), with its galleries, its fancy restaurant, and its Hammering Man. The Lusty Lady peep show and porn emporium used to be across the street, nicely tucked in next to the Harbor Steps hotel and apartment complex, but it closed down in 2010. The museum was built in the 1990s, with a design by famed postmodern Architect Robert Venturi, and most people felt that Venturi and Partners did their bit to uphold that previously quoted maxim, "Seattle is where good architects go to do their bad buildings." But a few years later somebody squeezed a lot of money out of bunch of millionaires and put together enough cash to have another architect—Brad Cloepfil, from Portland, Oregon—design a significant expansion of the relatively new building, with a new tower on top. These floors can be used to expand the museum as its collection grows.

Just down the street from the museum is the **⓬ Showbox** (1426 1st Avenue; www.showboxonline.com), one of the city's long-lived rock-and-roll clubs. Many great grunge bands played there back in the day, including Pearl Jam, and for those who love rock-and-roll, the Showbox books great music in a dozen different genres.

On the stretch of First Avenue south of the Seattle Art Museum is at least one historic musical address, 1214 1st Avenue, once occupied by a shop called Myers Music. This is where Jimi Hendrix bought his first electric guitar around 1958.

In the middle of downtown, the main branch of the Seattle Public Library (1000 4th Avenue; www.spl.lib.wa.us) is a bold silver-and-black oddball of a building that challenges preconceptions of what a "building" should look like, especially a major urban public library designed by world-renowned architect Rem Koolhaas. It opened to raves but has not necessarily aged well—there have been complaints about confusing floor plans, and the building materials are exhibiting signs of wear and tear already. But it's definitely worth a walk-through.

At the back end of downtown, where it begins to run up into Capitol Hill, a grand old theater called the Paramount (911 Pine Street; www.stgpresents.org/paramount) was refurbished in the 1990s by a Microsoft millionaire with money to burn and good taste. The place is an elegant mid-sized venue for rock-and-roll shows. Not exactly grungy, but very comfortable.

On the waterfront and reaching back into the city a block or two, Seattle's Olympic Sculpture Park (2901 Western Avenue; www.seattleartmuseum.org) is one of the great urban waterfront spaces on the West Coast. Zigging and zagging down a steep slope and over a couple of roads and railroad tracks, the park offers spectacular views framed by a fine collection of outdoor sculptures, including some sinuous hulks by Richard Serra and a giant Claes Oldenburg eraser.

Music fans might stroll by the nearby Edgewater Hotel (2411 Alaskan Way, Pier 67; www.edgewaterhotel.com), which has nothing to do with grunge, but is where the Beatles, the Rolling Stones, and Led Zeppelin stayed when they played Seattle. You could throw out a line and fish from the hotel room windows.

soundgarden

While Nirvana made its first inroads into Seattle in 1988, a band that already had been around a few years made historic inroads of a different sort. By 1988, after a few shifts in membership (reflecting the Seattle scene's informally communal musical style of the 1980s), Soundgarden consisted of Kim Thayil and Hiro Yamamoto, old friends from Illinois; Chris Cornell, a drummer who possessed an operatically large and compelling voice; and Scott Sundquist, a drummer brought in to free up Cornell for vocal duties. Sundquist soon quit, and was replaced by Matt Cameron from Skin Yard, another local band. In the wake of their contributions to the compilation *Deep Six*, Soundgarden became the first band to release an album on Sub Pop: the EP *Screaming Life*. The success of this EP inspired a follow-up EP, called *Fopp*. The buzz from these two Sub Pop records (Sub Pop later rereleased them together) got the attention of several major record labels, but the Soundgarden guys chose to stay faithful to their roots, for the moment at least, and signed a deal with the punk label SST in 1988. The band released an SST record called *Ultramega OK* that garnered further mainstream notice. Following this, the band signed with a major label, A&M Records, which put out the very first major label grunge LP, Soundgarden's hard-rocking *Louder than Love*. Although the personnel changes weren't quite complete—Hiro Yamamoto quit to attend pharmacy school and was replaced after a short interlude by Ben Shepherd—by the end of 1988, the band was on the verge of rock stardom.

shoreline

Louder than Love turned out to be the first of several significant grunge albums to be recorded at ⓭ **London Bridge Studio** (20021 Ballinger Way N.E., Shoreline; www.londonbridgestudio.com), a facility located in the north-of-Seattle town of Shoreline, Washington. This is a pleasantly woodsy suburban town with many charming residential neighborhoods, bordered on the west by Puget Sound and on three sides by three other towns. There is nothing to recommend it beyond its essentially sweet, unthreatening nature—and, perhaps, its fairly close connection to nature itself. But this studio had its fans—Pearl Jam and Alice in Chains also recorded classic early grunge classic records here. According to a *Seattle Times* story from 2005, by that year sales of albums made from London Bridge recordings numbered over 36 million.

The ⓮ Robert Lang Recording Studios (19351 23rd Ave N.W., Shoreline; www.robertlangstudios.com) is also in Shoreline, housed in a mammoth brickwork-finished structure on a hillside overlooking Richmond Beach. With its dramatic views of Puget Sound, this studio is a historically significant site in the grunge world, because it was here, in the last days of January 1994, that Nirvana did their last recording session. Aside from Nirvana, Dave Grohl's Foo Fighters, Alice in Chaines, Kenny G (!), Bush, Candlebox, Death Cab for Cutie, the Dave Mathews Band, and countless others have made records here since the studio opened in 1974.

Pearl Jam's Mike McCready talked about the Lang studio in an interview with the *Seattle Times*: "The studio just has this vibe to it. It's set in nature; you can look out the windows, and you can see Puget Sound, you can see the Olympics. . . . These are things that I notice in a studio. I can go outside and clear my head, instead of being downtown where you can't get away from it all. You can get away from it all up here, and then get back to work in the studio. It's just got this characteristic quirkiness to it."

This brings to mind that other aspect of Seattle's essence that mostly goes unmentioned in the grunge story, but that is certainly an indelible element in the soul of the northwest: stunning natural beauty and the ability to easily get into and experience it on a daily basis. For all the urban, dope-saturated angst of grunge, many of these guys were and still are country boys at heart.

mudhoney and sub pop

At the end of 1988, Mudhoney arrived. Sub Pop released *Re-hab Doll*, Green River's last EP, in June 1988; Mudhoney played its first two shows in July, opening for Blood Circus at the Vogue. A month later, the band released a seven-inch single titled "Touch Me I'm Sick" on Sub Pop. The song has demonstrated some staying power as a kind of grunge anthem. Mudhoney is still going strong, if sporadically extensively touring in 2015. Both of Mark Arm's seminal grunge bands, Mudhoney and Green River played sets at Sub Pop's twentieth anniversary concert/party, held at Marymoor Park in Redmond, Washington, in July 2008.

By the end of 1988, Sub Pop had released several more albums, singles, and compilations of songs from top Seattle bands. With its *Sub Pop 200* release in December of that year, the label was on its way to establishing itself as the definitive purveyor of the Seattle sound. Included in the boxed set were three twelve-inch EPs with twenty songs from twenty bands—all but one from Washington state. Bands featured included Mudhoney, Soundgarden, Green River, Blood Circus, Tad, Screaming Trees, Fastbacks, Swallow, and Nirvana.

In six days spanning the end of 1988 and early 1989, Nirvana went back into Reciprocal to finish recording the tracks that would eventually make up their first Sub Pop album, *Bleach*. With producer

Jack Endino at the dials, the thirty hours of sessions cost the band $606.17. A precursor of nightmares to come: as the story has it, the album title, *Bleach*, was chosen after Kurt Cobain saw a billboard advertising bleach as a way to clean and sterilize syringes used for shooting dope.

Grunge still standing (clockwise from top left): "Smells Like Teen Spirit" debuted live at the OK Hotel; several bands played early gigs at the bohemian Blue Moon Tavern; most of the characters in *Singles* lived in the Coryell Apartments; the Moore Theatre hosted many grunge bands; the Crocodile Cafe was the major grunge venue through the 1990s; the former home of Reciprocal Recording is where Nirvana (and hundreds of other grunge bands) recorded its first album.

chapter 4

the end of the innocence

The End of the Innocence, the title of a multimillion selling 1989 album by rock star (and former Eagle) Don Henley, aptly describes what happened in the grunge world at the tail end of the 1980s. Several home-grown Seattle grunge bands began competing with big-time rockers for spots atop the international pop music charts.

the british invasion, reversed

Toward the end of 1988, Sub Pop impresarios Bruce Pavitt and Jonathan Poneman, both serious students of the indie rock scene, made a fateful promotional decision. They recognized that one path toward success lay across the country and the pond, in Britain, where coverage from that country's rambunctious and lively musical press—*Melody Maker* and the *New Musical Express* being the main players—had in the past been the ticket to success for American musicians such as Jimi Hendrix and Blondie. Seeking a similar buzz for their Seattle bands, they paid for a British rock-and-roll journalist named Everett True to fly over to Seattle and report on the music scene for *Melody Maker*.

Everett True, born Jerry Thackray, published his first article about the Seattle scene—a story about Mudhoney—in March 1989 in *Melody Maker*. He raved about the Seattle scene, describing it as "the most vibrant, kicking music scene encompassed in one city for at least ten years."

True went on to spend years documenting the grunge scene, befriending many of the musicians and generally immersing himself in the Seattle musical world. He lived in Seattle on and off. He introduced Kurt Cobain to his future wife, Courtney Love, at a Butthole Surfers concert, and wheeled Cobain out on stage as a prank to open a Nirvana show in England. He wrote a book about Nirvana, and among the many insightful quotes he got from both Cobain and Courtney Love, this short one from Love offers a sharp psychological snapshot of Cobain: "Kurt was pure and he was also insanely ambitious. He just couldn't handle [fame]."

Not wanting to be outdone by the competition, the *New Musical Express* (where True had worked prior to his stint at *Melody Maker*) also went nuts over Seattle. And so, though the real explosion was still a ways off, the spring of 1989 marked the moment when grunge went international and Sub Pop began its transformation into a money-making record label.

One of the main events in this transformation was the release of Nirvana's *Bleach*, which came out on Sub Pop in June 1989. By then, the band had been touring for a few months with Chad Channing on drums. Ironically, since Nirvana's later records helped define the sound of grunge to much of the world, most Seattle musical insiders consider this first album to be the grungiest-sounding of all the band's albums. As Michael Azerrad explains it in his Nirvana book *Come As You Are*, for this first effort Cobain suppressed his pop musical instincts and made an album that would please the Sub Pop crowd.

Sub Pop also began promoting and putting on concerts. In June 1989, the label threw its first Lame Fest at the Moore Theatre in Belltown. The show featured Tad, Nirvana, and Mudhoney. Tickets were six bucks, and according to legend it was a great show except for the several fights that broke out in the audience.

About the Moore: the 1,419-seat **⑮ Moore Theatre** (1932 2nd Avenue; www.stgpresents.org/moore/history), added to the National Register of Historic Places in 1974, is a fine old venue located at 2nd Avenue and Virginia Street, where downtown Seattle eases into Belltown, the once-scruffy neighborhood immediately to the north. Built in 1907 (along with the adjacent Moore Hotel) for tourist entertainment and activities relating to the 1909 Alaska-Yukon-Pacific Exposition, the Moore later served as the original house theater for the Seattle International Film Festival when it was the Moore Egyptian Cinema in the 1970s. Don't be fooled by the simplicity of the tile and terracotta exterior—the building is a flamboyant celebration of Byzantine and Italianate styles.

In addition to hosting Lame Fest, the Moore has been a wonderful medium-sized venue for countless great rock-and-roll and grunge shows—Pearl Jam's "Even Flow" video footage was shot live at a 1992 concert there.

Meanwhile, toward the end of 1989, as Nirvana headed off to Europe on a short tour with Tad, future Pearl Jammers Stone Gossard and Jeff Ament's band Mother Love Bone signed a record deal with PolyGram, sending the band on its way to stardom, or so it seemed. They went into the London Bridge Studio in Shoreline, and got to work.

On January 6, 1990, the Gits, fronted by the gifted and charismatic Mia Zapata, opened for Tad and Nirvana in a notorious show at the HUB Ballroom at the University of Washington. Afterward, Cobain and Novoselic of Nirvana were banned for life from all university venues for destroying so much equipment. Those boys liked to smash things up.

ok hotel

The last decade of the twentieth century arrived in grunge Seattle with the opening of the ⑯ **OK Hotel** (212 Alaskan Way S.; no longer a music venue) on the edge of Pioneer Square in January 1990. The club was just small enough to escape the Teen Dance Ordinance, a repressive set of rules that had been put in place in 1985 after a club called the Monastery, run by some perverted religious creeps, got busted for feeding drugs and alcohol to homeless youth and then sexually abusing them, under the guise of running dances as religious services. The rules inspired by the Monastery case were far more repressive than necessary, and obviously designed to put the screws on Seattle's burgeoning rock-and-roll nightlife. Complete with onerous requirements for insurance, guards, and chaperones for minors, the ordinance essentially made it impossible to make money on shows for fans under twenty-one.

The OK Hotel would run as an all-ages venue for about four years, and then—perhaps when its core crowd grew up—it turned into a twenty-one-and-over nightclub. The OK was quite a scene in its day, and countless bands from the time played memorable shows there. Nirvana played "Smells Like Teen Spirit" live for the first time at the OK. Tad, Mudhoney, and Mother Love Bone played the OK. It also served as a significant location in Cameron Crowe's film *Singles*.

Damage from an earthquake in 2001 shut the building down. It was then repaired and earthquake-proofed, and reopened as the OK Hotel Apartments, with no coffee shop and no live music. You can peek in the windows and see paintings in the lobby areas where the coffee shops scenes in *Singles* took place, but the OK Hotel rocks no longer.

Early in 1990, Mother Love Bone played a show at the venerable ⑰ **Central Saloon** (207 1st Ave S.; www.centralsaloon.com), in Pioneer Square. There are several hundred-year-old bars in Pioneer Square, but the Central, open since 1892, hosted a number of great grunge shows in the 1980s and has been showcasing live rock-and-roll ever since. The Mother Love Bone show is significant, in retrospect, because it was the last show the band ever played. The band had recorded an album, *Apple*, for PolyGram Records, and had every expectation of attaining rock-and-roll stardom. On March 19, 1990, lead singer Andrew Wood died of a cerebral hemorrhage brought on by an overdose of heroin. And so as it turned out the album was released after his death. This is the day, many say, that grunge turned tragic. Wood was twenty-four years old and one of the most respected figures on the grunge scene.

Andrew Wood was born in 1966 in Columbus, Mississippi. After moving from Dallas, Texas, to Washington, he grew up on Bainbridge Island and formed Malfunkshun as a teenager with his brother Kevin. The only material Malfunkshun released was on the compilation *Deep Six* (C/Z Records).

Wood was much loved by his fans for his exuberant on-stage personality, his wild style of dressing, and his spacey lyrics. He started out imitating Robert Plant of Led Zeppelin, but later developed a more mature style reminiscent of Tommy Bolin. In *Hype!* Jack Endino calls Wood "the only stand-up comedian frontman in Seattle," a reference to Wood's always entertaining interaction with audiences.

A lyric sample from Mother Love Bone's "This Is Shangrila" sums up the pure pleasure Wood felt simply at being onstage:

get me to the stage—it brings me home again
this is Shangrila
i'm trippin' on it now—it brings me home again
this is Shangrila

With Wood's demise, the Seattle music community was forced to acknowledge that its innocence was lost and that heroin was now—or perhaps had always been—part of the scene.

pioneer square

Before plunging further in the 1990s, let's step back and take a quick tour of Pioneer Square. Along with the Central, other ancient bars in the square include the New Orleans (www.neworleanscreole-restaurant.com), the first saloon to open in rebuilt, postfire Pioneer Square in 1889; the (now closed) Doc Maynard's, named for that early purveyor of sin in Seattle; and the J&M (www.jandmcafe.com). They're all invitingly spacious, old-school saloons, layered with history. Photographer Charles Peterson, who maintains a studio in the neighborhood, recalls ordering take-out from a joint on 2nd and realizing that he was standing in what used to be the Metropolis, where so much happened twenty-five years before.

Seattle's great fire of 1889 turned out to be a blessing for Pioneer Square, as the neighborhood was rebuilt with an array of distinguished brick and stone buildings, many of which are still standing today. Prior to embarking on that major reconstruction, engineers solved the neighborhood's chronic drainage problems by elevating the street level a full story, leaving many original ground floors of buildings, and sidewalks, in subterranean catacombs that were sealed up and forgotten until the 1960s. That was when Seattle's business establishment, now entrenched a few blocks to the north, targeted the entire Pioneer Square district for urban renewal—essentially, they planned to tear it down and turn it into a collection of parking garages. They leveled the grand old Hotel Seattle and built the first of these garages in 1962. The appearance of this hideous structure gave the city's budding historic preservation movement a serious jumpstart, as did the Underground Tour of those hidden and forgotten prefire ground floors and sidewalks. The Underground Tour started up in 1964 and has been a vital part of the Seattle visitor circuit ever since (608 1st Avenue; www.undergroundtour.com). Today, Pioneer Square is the center of Seattle's art gallery scene; just to the south, you'll find the stadium homes of the Seattle Mariners and the Seahawks.

alice in chains breaks out

Another breakthrough album of 1990 was Alice in Chains' first full-length recording, *Facelift*. Having signed with Columbia in 1989, the band's initial release on that label was a promotional EP called *We Die Young*, featuring the single "Man in a Box." When this single became a hit on hard rock radio, Columbia rushed the band into production on *Facelift*. With Dave Jerden producing, the album was recorded at London Bridge Studios and released on August 21, 1990. Sales were slow at first, but after "Man in a Box" got into regular rotation on MTV, album sales took off, reaching 400,000 in six weeks and certified gold status by the end of the year.

This album as much as any other helped define grunge as, at least in part, an expression of alienation, depression, and—unsaid but very much in evidence—the painfully irresistible attraction of narcotics, specifically heroin. Alice in Chains guitarist Jerry Cantrell said the album's moody aura, most evident in the agonized vocals of Layne Staley, was a "direct result of the brooding atmosphere and feel of Seattle." Whether this moody aura qualified the band as grungy has been debated ever since. The grunge bands were all different, and Alice in Chains definitely had its own sound. Where this sound came from, and which subcategory it belongs to in the pop music scene, can be discerned, to some extent, from the bands that invited Alice in Chains to open their shows: Iggy Pop, Van Halen, Poison, and Extreme in 1990; in 1991, Alice in Chains opened the Clash of the Titans Tour, headlined by Slayer, Anthrax, and Megadeth. This is rock at its very hardest, with lyrics to match:

> I'm the man in the box
> Buried in my shit
> Won't you come and save me, save me
> Feed my eyes, can you sew them shut?

As Jerry Cantrell once said, "Our music's kind of about taking something ugly and making it beautiful."

the gestation of pearl jam

Heroin shadowed the musicians who would go on to form Pearl Jam as well, though in a different way. When an overdose killed Andrew Wood, Jeff Ament and Stone Gossard were emotionally devastated, for he was both band mate and good friend. They were also without a band. They went their separate ways for a short while, and Gossard began writing new songs and playing with another local guitarist, Mike McCready.

McCready was born in Florida in 1966 and moved to Seattle as a kid. He started playing guitar when he was eleven and formed his first band, Warrior, which soon changed its name to Shadow, while still in high school. After high school, the band went to LA to try to get a record deal but failed; they came back to Seattle and split up. McCready was ready to give up music until he attended a Stevie Ray Vaughan concert, got inspired, and started another band, Love Chile. His old friend Stone Gossard went to a Love Chile show, liked what he heard, and asked McCready if he'd like to start playing with him instead.

In time, McCready encouraged Gossard to reconnect with Ament, and the three began playing together. In search of a drummer and a lead singer, they put together a demo—recorded by Chris Hanzsek at Reciprocal—and sent it out to various friends and acquaintances. One guy they gave it to was former Red Hot Chili Pepper drummer Jack Irons. Irons passed on joining the new band—he was committed to his own band at the time—but he gave the tape to his basketball buddy, Eddie Vedder, who was living in the San Diego area and singing lead vocals for a local band called Bad Radio.

Vedder listened to the music, went surfing, and came up with lyrics to three songs that together tell the story of a kid who discovers he'd been lied to about who his father was and that his real father is dead. The kid grows up to be a serial killer, gets caught, and is sentenced to death. From the middle song, "Once":

Backstreet lover on the side of the road
I got a bomb in my temple that is gonna explode
I got a sixteen gauge buried under my clothes,
I play . . .
Once upon a time I could control myself

Vedder recorded vocals over the music and sent the tape back to Seattle. With writing credits going to Stone Gossard and Vedder, the songs were included on Pearl Jam's album *Ten*, released by Epic Records in August 1991.

McCready, Ament, and Gossard were so impressed by Vedder's work on the three songs—"Alive," "Once," and "Footsteps"—that they immediately flew him up to Seattle. Within a week he was in the band. Drummer Dave Krusen soon joined them. They called themselves Mookie Blaylock, after a professional basketball player they admired, and started practicing. Mookie Blaylock's first live performance was at a Seattle club called the **⑱ Off Ramp** (109 Eastlake Ave E.; www. elcorazonseattle.com), on October 22, 1990. Over the years, the Off Ramp was the scene of a number of great shows by all the bands in the grunge pantheon, and then some; it closed and reopened as Graceland, and had another run. More recently Graceland closed, and reopened as El Corazon, still doing live shows.

Eddie Vedder is yet another grunge star from a broken family—in his case, one with some unusual complications that he drew on for some of his early Pearl Jam lyrics, including the three songs on that legendary demo.

Vedder was born Edward Louis Severson III in the Chicago suburb of Evanston, Illinois, the son of Karen Lee (maiden name Vedder) and lounge singer Edward Louis Severson, Jr. His parents divorced in 1965, when he was a year old, and his mother soon married an attorney named Peter Mueller. Vedder was raised believing that Mueller was his biological father.

In the mid-1970s, the family, including Vedder's three younger half-brothers, moved to the San Diego area. Vedder took up guitar playing when he was twelve, and was an especially big fan of The Who. His mother and Mueller divorced when Vedder was in his late teens, and when his mother and brothers moved back to Chicago, Vedder stayed in California with his stepfather.

After this second divorce, Vedder learned that Mueller was really his stepfather. Vedder had met his biological father when he was a kid but was led to believe that Severson was an old friend of his parents. By the time Vedder learned the truth, Severson was dead. Vedder's already bad relationship with his stepfather got worse, and Vedder dropped out of San Dieguito High School in his senior year. He moved back to Chicago and changed his name to Eddie Vedder.

In 1984, Vedder returned to San Diego, where he started making demo tapes while working assorted low-rent jobs such as gas station attendant and security guard. He also played in various bands, ending up by 1990 as lead singer for Bad Radio. Then that demo arrived from Seattle via Jack Irons.

temple of the dog

In perhaps the ultimate tribute to Andrew Wood—and also honoring the Seattle scene's communal spirit—Chris Cornell of Soundgarden wrote several songs as a memorial to his deceased former roommate and then organized a tribute band with Mike McCready, Stone Gossard, Jeff Ament, and Soundgarden drummer Matt Cameron (who would end up in Pearl Jam after Soundgarden broke up seven years later). They named the Wood tribute band Temple of the Dog (from a Mother Love Bone song lyric) and recorded one album—Eddie Vedder, who had just arrived in town to join Mookie Blaylock, contributed backup vocals. Temple of the Dog performed live a few times, including one show at the Off Ramp in Seattle on November 13, 1990, just a few weeks after Mookie Blaylock debuted there.

Belatedly chasing after their savvy British counterparts, the knuckleheads at *Billboard*, the American music business publication, finally ran their Seattle story in August 1990: "At Long Last, Seattle Is Finally Hot," they announced, as if every rock-and-roll fan in the Western hemisphere didn't already know it. The story covered Nirvana, Soundgarden, Tad, the Walkabouts, and the Fluid.

the cascade

In September, Nirvana played a killer show at the **⓳ Motor Sports International Garage** (corner of Stewart Street and Yale Avenue N.; the building no longer exists) for an at-the-time huge crowd of fifteen hundred. This giant brick building was exactly that—a parking garage—except for a brief spell around 1990, when it became a rock-and-roll hall. The drummer for this Nirvana show was Dan Peters from Mudhoney. More important, one member of the audience was another drummer, Dave Grohl, whose East Coast band Scream had recently broken up. Novoselic and Cobain liked Grohl's style and had invited him to the show. He later said that he missed most of the Nirvana set—he spent it outside, talking with a friend—but nevertheless he auditioned for the band, and he was soon hired. This was just as Nirvana began to record demos for the album follow-up to the Sub Pop release *Bleach*. Grohl would be the last drummer in Nirvana.

The Off Ramp and the Motor Sports International Garage—and another contemporaneous club called **⓴ RKCNDY** (1812 Yale Avenue; closed)—were all located in a sort of (at the time) above-ground netherworld that some Seattleites refer to as the Cascade neighborhood. (Pearl Jam played at RKCNDY, and even Radiohead played shows there way back when. Eventually, RKCNDY closed; a hotel now occupies the site.)

Various punk and grunge clubs were situated amid the dirty concrete, harsh shadows, and grinding on and off ramps of the I-5 freeway at the foot of Capitol Hill just south of Lake Union, north of downtown. Closer to the foot of the hill (where the I-5 freeway slices through the heart of Seattle), shrinking pockets of well-tended single family residences can be found, and the beautiful Russian-looking onion-dome spires of St. Spyridon Cathedral still stand (not far from REI's massive flagship store, complete with glassed-in climbing wall). Yet during the twentieth century, this once-upon-a-time working-class residential area evolved into a motley assortment of warehouses, car dealerships, small factories, apartments, and mixed-use buildings.

In the 1990s, an effort was made to transform the area into a huge green space, a city park called the Seattle Commons, but public financing for this grand scheme was given the thumbs down by Seattle voters. Instead, commercial redevelopment came, and the Cascade, also known as South Lake Union, experienced a mixed-use building boom that lasted until the national real estate bubble burst in 2008. This boom was an inevitable occurrence, given the area's proximity to downtown Seattle, and though the recession slowed things down, the Cascade is another Seattle neighborhood that has been irrevocably changed.

As a result of Amazon's relocation into the neighborhood, development has been ongoing, intense, and relentless, with construction cranes ruling the sky and crowded streets below. With literally dozens of new skyscrapers under construction, South Lake Union—Cascadia—is the booming heart of the new Seattle.

But those particular booms were still in the distant future. In the world of grunge music, the big boom was just months away. On December 22, 1990, Mookie Blaylock played a show at the Moore Theatre. The other band on the bill that night was Alice in Chains.

Jack Endino, left, and Chris Hanzsek, seated, at Reciprocal Recording
soon after Reciprocal took over from Triangle Recording in the mid-1980s.
Among the bands who recorded at Reciprocal were
Nirvana, Soundgarden, and Green River.

Pearl Jam at Magnuson Park in 1992. The free show, an effort for Rock the Vote,
inspired thousands of people to register to vote. When Eddie Vedder tossed
the mic high above, it caught on scaffolding; he climbed up a pole
—hanging for a bit—and then slid down the cord.
He reportedly said early in the show,
"This is like the OK Hotel times one million."

chapter 5

the really big time

The break-out year on the grunge scene was 1991, with the major bands releasing hugely successful albums and hitting the big time in all possible ways. But the year began slowly.

pearl jam arrives

In the first couple months of 1991, Mookie Blaylock went down the West Coast as a supporting act for Alice in Chains. The two Seattle grunge bands played a series of club dates starting at the Off Ramp in Seattle, and including shows in Los Angeles, San Diego, San Francisco, Hollywood, Sacramento, and Portland. They were back in Seattle by the end of February.

Mookie Blaylock headed into London Bridge Recording Studios to begin making a new record on March 11, 1991, with Rick Parashar producing. With material on hand from earlier sessions and many of the songs already written, the recording took about a month. While they were in the studio, the threat of litigation from a lawyer representing basketball player Mookie Blaylock caused the band to change its name—to Pearl Jam. Eddie Vedder told a story about how the name came from his great-great-grandmother Pearl, who was married to a Native American and had a recipe for jam laced with peyote. This sounds like a great stoner tale, but it was revealed as just that—a stoner tale—when Vedder later admitted the story was "total bullshit" in an interview in *Rolling Stone* magazine. The first part of the name, Pearl, was Jeff Ament's idea, and Jam came to them collectively after they'd been to a Neil Young concert at which Young's band improvisationally stretched his songs out to fifteen or twenty minutes in length—this is called jamming, of course. Thus was born Pearl Jam.

Toward the end of the recording sessions in May, drummer Dave Krusen bailed on the band and checked himself into rehab, another Seattle musician fighting a bad habit. He was replaced, briefly, by Matt Chamberlain; when Chamberlain quit to join the Saturday Night Live band, he was replaced in turn by Dave Abbruzzese. The album they made that spring was called *Ten*, after Mookie Blaylock's basketball jersey number—they just couldn't give up on the guy! Like many of the grunge albums of the time, *Ten* is chock-full of fun songs about depression, alienation, loneliness, and murder.

This is one of the paradoxes of grunge: while so many of the songs from the period can be tortured downers, what people got from seeing these bands play—what the bands put out, onstage—was the opposite. The shows were celebrations, parties, carnivals. There was plenty of rage and mania, howling mad stage diving, and thrashing, but ask anyone if they had a good time at an early Pearl Jam or Nirvana show and the answer is always an unqualified YES! This is life-affirming music about anguish and rage.

belltown and the seattle club scene circa 1991

On April 12, 1991, a former lawyer by the name of Stephanie Dorgan opened a rock-and-roll club in Belltown, the semiscruffy neighborhood just north of downtown. The club was called the **㉑ Crocodile**

Café (2200 2nd Avenue; www.thecrocodile.com); the Posies (booked as POT, Posies on Tour) played opening night. The Croc would go on to become the central grunge nightclub of the 1990s (Stephanie Dorgan was married to Peter Buck of REM for a while).

Belltown was continually slated for all manner of major development, but that didn't transpire for years. For a good long stretch, Belltown (the original land claim for the area was made by a man named William Bell) was stuck in a downscale groove, home to a lot of small apartment buildings, cheap warehouses and manufacturing facilities, and generally useful if not particularly profitable businesses. Cheap rent, good spaces, close to downtown: Bohemia. And so Belltown became the place to go for good pool halls, movie theaters, affordable restaurants, bars, union halls, and a couple of grunge nightclubs, including the Weathered Wall (which reopened for music at the end of 2015), the Ditto Tavern, and the Croc.

Also of note in Belltown grunge lore is the **㉒ Black Dog Forge** (2316 2nd Avenue; www.blackdogforge.com). Both Pearl Jam and Soundgarden rehearsed in the basement, and the alley behind the Forge was a punker hangout.

Today, you can still party in Belltown like it's 1999. The neighborhood offers a number of good bars, restaurants, and other hangouts, although not as pleasantly downscale as they once were. The "new" **㉓ Cyclops Café** (2421 1st Avenue, www.cyclopsseattle.com) will never be as great as the original, but you still can walk down stretches of 1st or 2nd Avenue and find some authentically cool and grungy places to get wasted, waste money, or waste time. Bits of grunge Seattle are strewn all over Belltown. Don't miss the Two Bells Tavern (2313 Fourth Avenue), an authentic holdover from that earlier era.

rocking seattle

The self-titled *Temple of the Dog* album was released on April 16. It didn't sell too well in 1991, but a year later, after both Pearl Jam and Soundgarden had attained international stardom, A&M Records realized they had an informal collaboration between two of the world's most popular bands. The company rereleased it in 1992 and it went platinum, eventually selling over a million units.

On April 17, 1991, in a show at the OK Hotel, Nirvana played "Smells Like Teen Spirit" live for the first time.

In June, RKCNDY opened not far from the Off Ramp in the shadow of the I-5 Freeway. Seattle then had at least five clubs pretty much devoted to live rock-and-roll, especially of the grungy variety: the Vogue, the OK Hotel, the Crocodile Café, the Off Ramp, and RKCNDY. A couple of months later, local radio station KNDD, "The End," started playing new music by local bands. This was the first time in over three years that any Seattle radio station had played new, locally made music— another indicator of the rapidly rising influence of grunge.

big time albums

Then the albums arrived: Mudhoney's second album, *Every Good Boy Deserves Fudge,* was released by Sub Pop on July 26. Named for a mnemonic created to help students memorize the notes on the lines of the treble clef—EGBDF, with grungier "fudge" substituted for "favor"—the album is considered by many to be one of the best pure grunge albums recorded. Mudhoney moved to the major label Reprise Records the following year.

Pearl Jam's *Ten* was released by Epic Records on August 27. The record didn't do much initially, but in the long run it outsold Nirvana's *Nevermind,* the album that launched grunge into the rock-and-roll stratosphere.

nirvana conquers the world

After losing faith in Sub Pop—and maybe looking for a larger stage—the boys in Nirvana signed with David Geffen's DGC Records.

Shortly after signing the deal, they drove down to LA, where their next album was recorded in May and June at Sound City Studios in Van Nuys, with Butch Vig producing. *Nevermind* was released on DGC Records on September 14, 1991, debuting at 144 on Billboard's Top 200 album chart.

Historically speaking, *Nevermind* is the ultimate grunge album, at least in the collective memory of the rock-and-roll world. The underwater baby on the cover, swimming after a dollar bill and subject to multiple interpretations as well as the odd bit of absurd censorship—the baby's penis is visible!—lives on as an unforgettable visual icon of grunge.

Having gone through a couple of different drummers, on October 11, Nirvana played its first live show with Dave Grohl on drums. Toward the end of the year, the band headed off on a European tour to support the new album. However, when MTV put the music video for the album's first single, "Smells Like Teen Spirit," into major rotation, the record caught fire, and by Christmas 1991, it was selling 400,000 units per week.

The video for "Smells Like Teen Spirit" is a strangely compelling piece of work featuring the band performing the song before an audience of seemingly alienated high schoolers (a bunch of kids recruited via announcements on a local college radio station); the gym is obviously a set (constructed on a sound stage in Culver City, California); the cheerleaders, with anarchy symbols on their uniforms, look robotic; the janitor is played by a real janitor; and the whole thing ends with a slow-motion audience slam dance into destruction of the set. The thing is weird, but Kurt Cobain, a shadowy figure throughout, gets his close-up at the end—and was immediately transformed into a charismatic rock star.

Life would never be the same for him. Or for flannel shirts—he wore one in the shoot, and thus grunge fashion arrived on the world stage. Also arriving on the strength of this video was the "who gives a fuck?" attitude of grunge—the audience in the video clip is being crooned to by a budding rock star and looks decidedly uninterested in what he's doing.

But everybody else became interested in what Kurt Cobain was doing. Grunge madness had begun. The European shows were oversold, "Smells Like Teen Spirit" became omnipresent in media land, and TV crews began following the band everywhere.

Ironically, although Nirvana embodied the visual ideal of grunge, many of the songs on this album are actually more pop rock in style than sludgy, heavy-duty grunge—especially the anthem "Smells Like Teen Spirit." Cobain probably had more in common with John Lennon and Paul McCartney than he did with Robert Plant, Ozzy Osbourne, or even Eddie Vedder or Chris Cornell.

soundgarden's turn

Recorded in March and April in studios in California and Washington, *Badmotorfinger*, the second full-length album from Soundgarden, was released on A&M Records on October 8. Although the album was overshadowed by the frenzy surrounding Nirvana over the next few months, it is considered by critics to be something of a masterpiece, featuring odd time signatures, arty, inventive musical touches, and an experimental quality not expected from a grunge supergroup verging on commercial success and stardom. Yet the record is totally accessible and commercial at the same time. That was the brilliance of Soundgarden. The record is also the first Soundgarden album with bassist Ben Shepherd, and the other band members acknowledged that Shepherd's playing and writing skills elevated the band to a new level. The album eventually peaked at thirty-nine on the *Billboard* chart and went double platinum.

seattle ascendant

In November 1991, *Spin* magazine included four Seattle bands in its top ten albums of the year: Nirvana's *Nevermind*, Pearl Jam's *Ten*, Soundgarden's *Badmotorfinger*, and Mudhoney's *Every Good Boy*

Deserves Fudge. Mudhoney, the stepchild of grunge and still signed to Sub Pop Records, was hanging in there with the big boys—though the band would move to a major label the next year.

When *Nevermind* hit number one on the Billboard chart on January 11, 1992 (the album also hit number one in seven other countries and the top three in several others), grunge had irrevocably arrived, which meant, more or less, that the underground or indie music scene had buried the major label, heavily promoted glam and arena rock scene of the 1980s. Several bands had paved the way for the indie phenomenon, including REM, Sonic Youth, and Black Flag, but with the astounding commercial success of *Nevermind*, the playing field changed. The anticommercial, do-it-yourself, independent grunge movement had taken over the commercial pop music world.

seattle descending

Or grunge was officially dead, depending on your perspective. In the minds of a contingent of purists, grunge died with the suicide of local writer Steven Jesse Bernstein on October 29, 1991.

Bernstein was an LA kid who moved to Seattle and began performing as an opening act for many grunge bands in the early years of the scene. A heavy abuser of all kinds of dope, he was notorious and admired for the antisocial, intense, stoned, and perverse nature of his live performances, which included such moves as urinating on audience members, reciting poetry with a live rat in his mouth, and flinging bottles, food, and other objects at the crowd. At one point he went into a Washington state prison to record a live album for Sub Pop. The recording, *Prison*, was scored with jazz and ambient music by producer Steve Fisk; it was released on April 1, 1992, after Bernstein's death. Bernstein committed suicide by stabbing himself three times in the throat. He was forty years old.

One piece from the prison recording made it into the soundtrack for Oliver Stone's notorious film *Natural Born Killers*. Bernstein's book, *I Am Secretly an Important Man*, was published in 1996 by Zero Hour Publishing.

singles

Long-time *Rolling Stone* writer and successful filmmaker Cameron Crowe wrote and directed the one fictional film that ties directly into the grunge scene just before its peak. *Singles* stars Bridget Fonda, Matt Dillon, Kyra Sedgwick, and Campbell Scott, and features performances and cameo appearances from members of Soundgarden, Pearl Jam, Alice in Chains, and several other grunge bands from Seattle and elsewhere. Although the film is not about grunge per se, the final version of the script Crowe shot was inspired by the death of singer Andy Wood and the gathering of musicians and friends that happened in the wake of that tragedy. He started thinking about the grunge scene as a community that day—about how people instinctively need to be together—and it helped him transform the script. The film was shot in 1990 and 1991, but was not released until 1992, at which point grunge had hit the big time and the movie and record companies realized what they had on their hands: a film with a soundtrack featuring songs from several of the biggest bands in the world. It also had members of the same bands playing live in the film as well as showing up in cameos.

The movie includes scenes shot in the now-defunct coffee shop at the OK Hotel as well as concert footage at RKCNDY. Other scenes take place at Gasworks Park on Lake Union in Seattle (a great urban park with a killer view of downtown Seattle), the Jimi Hendrix grave and memorial in Renton, Pike Place Market, and an apartment complex on Capitol Hill that is home sweet home for the main players in the story.

The film has aged rather well. When it arrived, fans of Crowe's earlier work were somewhat disappointed at the offbeat, understated style of the movie—the narrative advances in chapters, like a novel, and is essentially a small, well-told story about regular people struggling to connect, to not remain single. This is fine, but the whole thing feels underplayed—especially when the dramatic leads find themselves in nightclubs, standing stock still and murmuring offbeat throwaway lines while Alice in Chains or Soundgarden thrash through a tune onstage twenty feet away. The onstage musical angst is heavy and dramatic, while the characters meander through their troubled yet sweet interactions without ever even raising their voices.

However, in retrospect, the movie is a pleasure to watch, perhaps because the main musical character, a grunge dude named Dick, is played so very well as a loveable if self-involved lunkhead by Matt Dillon. The dramatic narrative feels true: sweet, down to earth, and touching—especially in light of what Crowe noted about rewriting the script after Andrew Wood's death.

Some kick-ass concert footage is included, as are cameos—some good, some not so good—from several later-to-be major grunge stars, including Eddie Vedder, Stone Gossard, and Jeff Ament from Pearl Jam and Chris Cornell from Soundgarden. The scenes were shot when these guys were on the verge of hitting the big time.

Watching *Singles* now is something of an exercise in nostalgia, for the music of course, but also for the mood. Grunge may have been an angst-ridden musical style, but the Seattle in the movie feels a lot warmer, mellower, and more comfortable than the hectic, paranoid, traffic-crazed city of Seattle circa 2016—mellower for musicians and for everybody else. The sense of community is a powerful subtext in this movie, affecting both the musicians and the characters in the fictional story. Incidentally, the character played by Campbell Scott is a humble bureaucrat—a traffic planning specialist—with a utopian vision of mass transit.

here come the tabloids!

On February 22, 1992, during a Nirvana tour of the Pacific Rim, Kurt Cobain married Courtney Love on the beach at Waikiki in Honolulu, Hawaii, formalizing a relationship that seemingly caused both of them a lot of pain along with whatever marital bliss they found. They had briefly met in Oregon in 1989, and after meeting again at a Butthole Surfers show in LA when Nirvana was there in 1991 recording *Nevermind*, they began a serious courtship that for quite a while involved much long-distance yakking and occasional getting together and, apparently, doing dope. They were attracted to each other, of course, but for these two, falling in love initially meant, "We bonded over pharmaceuticals," as Love told Michael Azerrad in *Come as You Are*. They both had a hankering for opiates—heroin, morphine, codeine, opium, hydrocodone—the usual bad shit on the downer end of the drug scale that unfortunately seemed to be the habit of choice for many a grunger. Cobain used pain-killing meds for chronic stomach and back pain, which he suffered from for years—but with hard drugs, there is use and there is abuse, and clearly Cobain lived on both sides of that murky gray line.

In any case, Courtney, lead singer and muse of a highly respected (especially in the crit-heavy UK), hard-rocking, angry grrrl band called Hole, and Kurt, budding major rock star, tied the knot on the beach in Hawaii. There are those in the know who will always be convinced that she drove him to the brink—and over. But that was later. In 1992, Nirvana conquered the world, and Courtney Love got on the train and went along for the ride.

In September 1992, a month after Courtney gave birth to Frances Bean Cobain (Kurt was passed out and missed the event), *Vanity Fair*'s profile of the pregnant and strung-out Love and her marriage to Cobain appeared. It was a scandalous piece, painting her as conniving, nasty, and selfish—as well as doing drugs while pregnant. Not a pretty picture, even if Frances did turn out to be a healthy and happy young woman (she looks strikingly like her father). Healthy baby or not, heroin was now formally a character in the grunge story.

alice in chains conquers all

Following their success with *Facelift* and their extensive 1991 tour, Alice in Chains went back into the studio late in 1991 to record demos for a new album. While in the studio, as the story has it, drummer Sean Kinney dreamed that they made an acoustic EP called *Sap*, so called because the songs were sappy, according to Kinney. The band decided to obey the dream. The five-song acoustic EP *Sap* was released on March 21, 1992, when Nirvana's *Nevermind* ruled the *Billboard* charts, thrusting Seattle bands into the international limelight. *Sap* features Ann Wilson from Heart singing back-up on three songs and musical guest appearances from Mark Arm of Mudhoney and Chris Cornell of Soundgarden. It quickly went gold.

Even before this record was released, Alice in Chains went back into the studio in February 1992 to record another album. Written during the band's earlier tours and also in the studio, many of the album's twelve tunes move into a decidedly darker realm—the realm of addiction, which was becoming an increasingly intense problem for various members of the band. Released in September 1992, *Dirt* peaked at six on the *Billboard* chart, garnered critical acclaim, and has gone multiplatinum in the years since.

lollapalooza

In spite of all the druggy vibes, the grunge juggernaut rolled on. One indicator of the rising importance of the scene—not only commercially but in terms of alternative music and alternative culture buzz— was the way the line-up for Perry Farrell's Lollapalooza Festival changed from 1991 to 1992. Originally conceived as a farewell tour for Farrell's band, Jane's Addiction, the traveling rock-and-roll festival became an annual gathering of the tribes for youth culture throughout the 1990s. Lollapalooza rocked! From its inception in 1991 until its first demise six years later (there was a revival in 2003), the show featured great, critically acclaimed, commercially successful bands of all kinds on the main stage, up and comers on the second stage, all accompanied by a bevy of socially and politically progressive speakers, companies, causes, and weird sideshow acts such as the Jim Rose Circus.

In 1991, not a single Seattle band was on the roster. In 1992, along with non-Seattle headliners Ice Cube, the Jesus and Mary Chain, Lush, and the Red Hot Chili Peppers, main stage acts from Seattle included Ministry (hard rock), Pearl Jam, and Soundgarden. On the second stage, Seattle acts included Chris Cornell and Eddie Vedder (a side performance for the two lead singers) and the Jim Rose Circus. The 1992 festival played in Washington state just once, at the Kitsap County Fairgrounds (1200 NW Fairgrounds Rd, Bremerton; www. kitsapgov.com/parks/Fairgrounds/Pages/Fair_Main_Page.htm) across Puget Sound from Seattle.

mudhoney revisited

Seattle's original grunge band, Mudhoney, never made it as big as the four bands featured in this book, but they did sign a major label deal with Reprise Records—everything else they'd done was on Sub Pop—and late in 1992 released *Piece of Cake*, a collection that received mixed reviews and was described by some critics as more like garage rock than grunge. Whatever it was, it did not turn them into the superstars that many of their peers had become. In spite of this—and in spite of the fact that members of several bands whose sound and style grew out of Mudhoney and its predecessor, Green River, became millionaire rock-and-roll stars—the members of Mudhoney have persisted, disbanding here and there but seemingly always driven to reunite for another album or another tour.

They might be described as the anti-Pearl Jam, in terms of commercial success. There is some irony in that description, because two guys in Pearl Jam came from the same band as two guys in Mudhoney—Green River.

Things took a negative turn in May 1992, when Seattle's Parks and Recreation Department revoked a previously issued permit allowing Pearl Jam and a punk band called Seaweed to play a "Rock the Vote" concert in ㉔ **Gasworks Park** (2101 N. Northlake Way) on the shore of Lake Union in Seattle. The concert was intended to promote voter registration among young people, but the city fathers got scared at the thought of 30,000 kids packed into the park for a rock-and-roll show. Eddie Vedder later said, "It wasn't the NUMBER of people that bothered them, it was the TYPE of people—30,000 YOUNG people, 30,000 ALTERNATIVE people." The band subsequently planned a different event, "Drop in the Park," which took place a few months later, on September 20, at Magnuson Park, a larger Seattle city park on the shore of Lake Washington (not far from where the Soundgarden namesake sculpture can be found). Drop in the Park performers included Pearl Jam, Cypress Hill, Pete Droge, Seaweed, and the Jim Rose Circus, along with featured speaker Robert Anton Wilson, a semi-underground American writer and philosopher. Wilson is renowned in alternative cultural circles, particularly for his *Illuminatus!* trilogy, published in 1975 and advertised as "a fairy tale for paranoids."

the good, the bad, and the just plain silly

Between May and September of 1992, grunge as a cultural phenomenon hit its stride. On June 26, the soundtrack to *Singles* was released, with songs from all the major grunge bands (except Nirvana, for Kurt Cobain was said to have hated the movie) and several individual band members in diverse collaborative efforts. Two days later, another heroin-induced Seattle rock-and-roll tragedy occurred with the death of twenty-two-year-old Stefanie Sargent, the guitarist in the rocking girl band 7 Year Bitch. In one of those luridly unforgettable events, Sargent died by choking to death on her own vomit after drinking a lot of alcohol and then taking heroin.

Sargent's death represented the tragic side of things that fateful summer. In the fall, just before the Drop in the Park show, the sublimely ridiculous side of the grunge phenomenon found its expression in, of all places, the *New York Times*. On September 15, the *Times* reprinted a so-called Glossary of Grunge that had been published in the British magazine *Sky International*. This "glossary" had been obtained by a reporter who called Sub Pop Records to find out just what this grunge business was all about. The girl who answered the phone, Megan Jasper (who now manages Sub Pop!), proceeded to give the guy a list of grunge words that she made up on the spot. Grunge terms, according to the *Times*, included brilliant items such as cob nobbler (loser), lamestain (an uncool person), wack slacks (old, ripped jeans), and swingin' on the flippity flop (hanging out). Jasper wonderfully explains this whole scam in the movie *Hype!*, but in general, this fake glossary—revealed as such three months later in the Chicago-based magazine *The Baffler*—sums up the put-on side of the grunge scene. *The Baffler* wrote, in revealing the hoax, that "when the Newspaper of Record goes searching for the Next Big Thing and the Next Big Thing piddles on its leg, we think that's funny." People on the scene in Seattle knew the whole thing was a huge joke. Members of Mudhoney even began using the fake words during interviews.

The apotheosis of grunge as ridiculous cultural phenomenon was attained in December 1992, when *Vogue* magazine ran its "Grunge and Glory" fashion spreads, with $500 to $1,400 "grunge outfits" styled by top New York designers mimicking the look "coming out of the clubs, garages, and thrift shops of Seattle." RIP, grunge.

gathering clouds

By 1993, grunge and the Seattle scene had attained international renown and recognition as a bona fide cultural phenomenon. In 1992 and 1993, record company reps, promoters, and all manner of corporate buzz-killers swarmed into Seattle, signing dozens of Seattle bands to record deals in the hopes of discovering the next Nirvana.

Meanwhile, the real thing, Nirvana, led by the sporadically strung-out and generally troubled Kurt Cobain, played some international dates. Cobain did a cover story interview in the *Advocate*, a magazine devoted to gay culture, further feminizing his already somewhat androgynous image. The band went to Minnesota to work with producer Steve Albini on a new record, which would end up being *In Utero*. The band was unhappy with some of the mixes, and another producer was brought in to remix several songs, which led to a lot of press chatter about the band's selling out or being sold out by their record label. The volume on this babble was ratcheted up a few decibels when rumor had it that executives from the record label DGC supposedly thought the album was "unreleasable." As it turned out it was very releasable, but . . . it is a schizophrenic piece of work, full of hope and optimism on the one hand—falling in love, getting married, and having a baby can do that—and full of anger and fundamental alienated despair on the other. Those kinds of bad feelings—despair, rage, depression—were part of the deal for a chronically tortured and oft-strung-out Kurt Cobain with a chronically crazed and strung-out wife like Courtney Love. From the song "Serve the Servants":

> Teenage angst has paid off well
> Now I'm bored and old
> Self-appointed judges judge
> More than they have sold

The record contains and expresses the paradoxes of grunge: loud, raw, rock-and-roll, fuzz and feedback and angry noise, pretty pop melodies. *In Utero* debuted at number one on the Billboard chart in September 1993, although in the end it didn't do as well as *Nevermind*.

Following a US tour in the fall, the band went to New York to video-tape a live performance for *MTV Unplugged*. Shot at the Sony Studios in New York City, the show aired on MTV on December 14, 1993.

After a grueling year primarily spent touring, Soundgarden slowed down a little in 1993. Band members all engaged in side projects; they released *Motorvision*, a homemade video of concert footage from the 1991 and 1992 tours. Toward the end of the year, the band returned to the studio to begin work on its next album, to be released in 1994, called *Superunknown*.

With a new bassist, Mike Inez, in place, and two songs on the soundtrack for the Arnold Schwarzenegger action parody film *Last Action Hero*, Alice in Chains in 1993 seemingly had entrenched themselves in the monied mainstream. Then they joined the Lollapalooza Festival for the summer tour. This ended up being the last tour the band made with Layne Staley singing lead vocals. Late in 1993, the band went back into the studio to do some acoustic recording. They spent just a week at it, producing an EP called *Jar of Flies* that was released in January 1994.

pearl jam triumphant

While 1992 surely will be remembered as the year of Nirvana, Pearl Jam owned 1993. The band had toured relentlessly in support of their 1992 album *Ten*, jammed on *MTV Unplugged*, joined Lollapalooza for the summer, and played on *Saturday Night Live*. Although they were derided by Kurt Cobain as a corporate band dressed in grunge clothing, Pearl Jam was an unstoppable force thanks to Eddie Vedder's tortured, soulful singing. They won several MTV Video Awards for "Jeremy," but refused to make a video for their other hit single, "Black," on the grounds that they wanted to be remembered for their songs, not for the images that went along with them.

They released their next album, *Vs.*, on October 19, 1993. The record sold an astonishing 950,378 copies in its first week of release, outpacing the combined sales of all the other albums on Billboard's Top Ten for the week. In response to all this success, the band declined to make any more music videos, stopped talking to the press, and pushed promoters to put a cap on ticket prices for the band's tours. They were trying to keep it real! In the final, welcome-to-the-big-time coup de grace, Eddie Vedder appeared on the cover of *Time* magazine on October 25, 1993, as the iconic tortured young grunge rock star. Vedder and the members of Pearl Jam had not talked to the magazine's reporters, and Vedder was reportedly not at all thrilled to be on the cover.

a violent death shakes up the scene

Earlier in the year, a more seriously tragic event took place in the Seattle music scene when Mia Zapata, the gifted and charismatic lead singer of the Gits, was raped and murdered while walking home from a Capitol Hill bar called the ㉕ **Comet Tavern** (922 E. Pike Street; thecomettavern.com).

The Comet is a great old bar and longtime night crawler hangout that unfortunately has that one dark mark in its history. Zapata left the Comet late on the night of July 7, 1993, heading home after an evening hanging out with friends, who had gathered to commemorate the death of Stefanie Sargent a year earlier. Rather than stay with a friend who lived nearby or take a cab ride home, she decided to walk the mile and a half to her own place. She never made it. Her body was found halfway between the bar and her apartment.

In the wake of Zapata's murder, a self-defense group called "Home Alive" was formed, funded by benefit concerts and CDs featuring

Seattle rockers, including Nirvana, Pearl Jam, Heart, Soundgarden, and the Presidents of the United States of America. Utilizing DNA evidence, her killer was identified in Florida in 2003. A year later, more than ten years after her death, he was convicted of murder.

Mia Zapata was born in Louisville and formed her band, the Gits, while attending college at Antioch in Yellow Springs, Ohio. The band moved to Seattle in 1989 because that's where bands went in those days. The Gits became an integral part of the Seattle scene, though they were more feminist rockers than grungesters. The Gits are captured live in *Hype!*, where Zapata's talent and charismatic stage presence are fully on display.

capitol hill rocks on

Capitol Hill, where this scary, tragic event occurred, has long been an integral part of the Seattle hipster scene. Several clubs and bars are still standing that started out before or during the grunge years. Just up the block from the Comet, around 10th Avenue and Pike Street in the heart of commercial Capitol Hill, is the rock-and-roll bar called **26 Neumos** (925 E. Pike Street; www.neumos.com). This joint opened originally in the early nineties as Moe's Mo' Rockin' Café, or Moe for short, and its main stage was the scene for a number of great grunge shows and concerts, including a now-legendary 1995 Neil Young–Pearl Jam collaboration that wrapped a whole lot of rock-and-roll history into a couple of loud, mind-blowing nights. Neumos continues to showcase established and up-and-coming rock-and-roll acts.

Not far from there, on the Broadway side of the corner of Pine Street and Broadway, across the street from the campus of Seattle Central Community College (one of several colleges in the neighborhood whose presence contributes to the lively street scene), is a statue of Jimi Hendrix playing his guitar (900 East Pine Street).

Farther east on Capitol Hill are the **❷❼ Coryell Apartments** (1820 E. Thomas Street). This nondescript, slightly dingy yet pleasant courtyard apartment building served as the primary location for *Singles*. Several of the main characters in the film live in this complex, and much of the film's action takes place in the little central courtyard and in several apartments.

by the way #4

singles songs and characters

When Chris Cornell of Soundgarden saw the list of song titles, by the fictional band Citizen Dick, made up by Jeff Ament for the movie *Singles* (the list appears briefly in the film), he decided to write real songs to match each made-up song title. One of these songs, "Seasons," appears on the film soundtrack. Another is "Spoonman," which Soundgarden later recorded. The song is about, and features, Artis the Spoonman, a well-known Seattle street musician. It became a hit in 1994, and a rough version can be heard in the movie.

The rock-and-roll character played by Matt Dillon, leader of the band Citizen Dick, is loosely based on Jeff Ament (Dillon reportedly borrowed much of his wardrobe for the movie from Ament). The band has one tune called "Touch Me, I'm Dick," which is a wordplay on "Touch Me, I'm Sick" by Mudhoney.

Actors making brief or cameo appearances in the film include Eric Stoltz (as the mime); Victor Garber; Jeremy Piven (he hit the big time years later on the HBO series *Entourage*); Paul Giamatti; Seattle local Tom Skerritt, who plays the mayor; and film director Tim Burton. Cameron Crowe also makes an appearance as an interviewer in a club.

by the way #5

the jim rose circus

One of the stranger nonmusical acts to emerge from the early nineties scene in Seattle was the Jim Rose Circus, a postmodern collection of sideshow freaks whose masochistic performances struck a common chord with the grunge crowd.

In the often seemingly endless intermission between shows on a given night in a given club, while the roadies break down one band's batch of gear and set up another's, the crowd needs something to do other than get wasted. So bring on the circus! Why not watch a guy lift a keg of beer with a cord pinned to his tongue, his left nipple, or even his penis?

Historically, sideshows have been off to the side, slightly hidden, where people can sneak over and watch creepy stuff that is somehow . . . sexy. Compelling. Irresistible. Hey, people get off on all manner of weird shit, and weird shit has always been hanging around backstage in the world of rock-and-roll.

One need only look as far as Iggy Pop, of Stooges fame, to find a rock-and-roll star whose onstage antics include rolling in broken glass, some provocative work with burning cigarettes, and stage-diving into the occasional missed catch. Iggy and his kind were a big influence on the grunge scene, and many can remember Eddie Vedder, Chris Cornell, Kurt Cobain, and others flinging themselves around and off of stages, amplifiers, and other perches, possessed by the spirits of musical and lyrical frenzy.

But Jim Rose and his crew took the notion of onstage pain as performance a little further. They organized, dolled up, and nearly mainstreamed some intensely masochistic stage business. Masochistic, but very entertaining indeed.

After working the grunge circuit in Seattle in the early nineties, Rose and company hit the big time when the Jim Rose Circus Sideshow got booked on the side stage for Perry Farrell's Lollapalooza Tour in 1992. The Jim Rose Circus also performed as an opening act on Trent Reznor's Nine Inch Nails tour in 1994.

Rose has played countless venues since, although his act will never quite be ready for prime time, as it were. Not network prime time, anyway. It is just too . . . well, scary is one way of putting it, to watch people do what his people do. But he's definitely a star of a sort; he and one of his main guys, the Enigma, made a memorable appearance on one of the strangest episodes of *The X Files* (the episode "Humbug"). Come to think of it, that was prime time! As was Rose's appearance on *The Simpsons*, when Homer tried out for a spot in the Jim Rose Circus as the Human Cannonball.

Jim Rose grew up in Phoenix, Arizona, where as a kid he was drawn to hanging out with circus sideshow people. Eventually he went to Europe, where the small circus and its stable of sideshow oddities remains a living tradition. There, Rose learned a few tricks—"The Bed of Nails" and "Regurgitation"—before returning to the states and beginning his professional career on that most public of stages, the Venice Beach boardwalk in Los Angeles. From LA he made his way to Seattle. The rest is history.

Back in the grunge years, the Jim Rose cast of characters included:

Slug (Paul Lawrence) the man who would eat anything, including worms and grasshoppers. He also swallowed swords. Eventually, he had his body completely covered with blue tattoos of jigsaw puzzle pieces, had horns implanted in his head, and renamed himself the Enigma. At last report, more than two hundred different tattoo artists had worked on him. The Enigma, it should be said, is also an accomplished musician, actor, and man about the stage, with a full schedule of personal appearances.

The Amazing Mister Lifto (Joe Hermann) lifted heavy objects such as steam irons, cinderblocks, even beer kegs on lines attached to his body piercings. The locations of these piercings included nipples and genitalia. The "Genital Lift" was always a "cover your eyes and peek between your fingers" kind of crowd favorite.

The Tube (Matt Crowley) was so named for his ability to swallow up to seven feet of tubing. The unswallowed end of the tube was attached to a hand pump, and Jim Rose would fill the pump with all manner of fluids, then pump it into the Tube's stomach. The coup de grace came when Rose pumped the same fluid out of the Tube's stomach and invited audience members up to drink the stuff. Those who had already ingested several quarts, if not gallons, of beer were generally the only ones to meet this disgusting challenge. If no one stepped up, the Tube would redrink it himself. He also demonstrated his freakish lung power by blowing air into a hot water bottle until it exploded.

Bebe the Circus Queen (Beatrice Aschard) had an act that included having a watermelon placed on her back and then split with a saber, lying on a bed of nails and having weights placed on her chest, and the ever-popular "Plastic Bag of Death," wherein she climbed inside a huge plastic bag and then another member of the show sucked all the air out of the bag. Bebe, who is French, is married to the man himself, Jim Rose.

Zamora the Torture King (Tim Cridland) pierced himself with skewers and long needles, walked up and down a ladder with razor-sharp blades for rungs, ate pieces of broken light bulb (with a microphone by his mouth so the crowd could hear him chew), and held a fluorescent lamp in one hand while touching a generator. The lamp would glow. Torture King went on to start his own act, and has been on the road ever since.

Jim Rose, in addition to his duties as ringmaster and impresario, occasionally drove long nails up his nose, stapled money to his forehead, and invited audience members to stand on his head after he'd placed it in a box of broken glass.

Other acts over the years have included Mexican Transvestite Dwarves, the Armenian Rubberman (who slipped his entire body through a tennis racket), Lesbian Sumo Wrestlers, and dozens of other weirdos. You get the picture. It is disturbing, but undeniably entertaining. The Jim Rose Circus is still going strong. They've performed—and have been threatened with bans against performing—all over the world. In other media, Rose has published several books and acted in a number of films. His work, as well as that of the circus and all related activities, can be tracked on a very lively website, www.jimrosecircus.com.

Alice in Chains' Layne Staley on stage at the Paramount
Theater in 1993.

Soundgarden's Chris Cornell stage diving into the crowd during a 1992 Lollapalooza show. The lineup included Pearl Jam and the Jim Rose Circus.

At the memorial for Kurt Cobain in April 1994, the crowd celebrated not his death but his life.

chapter 6

fade out

By 1994, having conquered the musical world, more or less, grunge as a movement had nowhere to go but down. In that year and in future years, several albums by the bands discussed here, along with assorted knock-offs, imitators, wannabes, and others, would sell in the millions, making a few dozen young Seattle dudes into wealthy rock stars, but the downward spiral had begun. As has been said many times and in many places, "Money changes everything." It definitely changed grunge.

In January 1994, Nirvana went into the Robert Lang Recording Studios in Shoreline to begin work on new recordings. Shortly thereafter, they headed off on a tour of Europe.

On January 25, 1994, Columbia Records released *Jar of Flies*, the acoustic EP Alice in Chains had recorded in one week late in 1993. The collection became the first-ever EP to debut at number one on the Billboard 200. The music got raves. Paul Evans of *Rolling Stone* called the EP "darkly gorgeous." *Jar of Flies* includes "No Excuses," grunge's only number one single on mainstream rock charts. The second single, "I Stay Away," reached number ten, while the final single, "Don't Follow," reached number twenty-five. The band was scheduled to go on tour with Metallica and Suicidal Tendencies in the summer of 1994, but apparently Layne Staley started using hard drugs again during rehearsals, and the band was forced to withdraw from the tour.

On March 15, 1994, A&M Records released *Superunknown*, a new album from Soundgarden. The album debuted at number one on the Billboard 200, got rave reviews from rock critics across the country and around the world, and eventually went quintuple platinum, solidifying Soundgarden's mid-nineties claim as one of the top rock-and-roll bands in the world—and a band with an experimental bent, for this record, like Soundgarden's earlier albums, does far more than play with heavy metal tropes. It incorporates Beatlesque influences, weird tunings, Middle Eastern undercurrents, and richly evocative lyrics that conjure the paradoxes and perils of rock-and-roll success (and human existence) as well as anything from Nirvana or Pearl Jam. (Chris Cornell claims to have been reading the haunted, suicidal poet Sylvia Plath while writing lyrics.) The album spawned three hit singles and a couple of award-winning videos. It was nominated for a Best Rock Album Grammy in 1995, and is anumber 335 on *Rolling Stone* magazine's 500 Greatest Albums of All Time.

the death of kurt cobain

In March, Nirvana headed across the pond for a brief European tour. The first signs of trouble came when Kurt Cobain was diagnosed with severe laryngitis and bronchitis and had to cancel a show in Munich. In Rome on March 4, Courtney Love found Cobain unconscious. He was hospitalized, and the doctors told the press he'd fallen into a coma after eating fifty tablets of rohypnol, a depressant, which he apparently washed down with a bottle of champagne. The rest of the tour was cancelled. After five days in the hospital, Cobain was released and flew home to Seattle. On March 18, Courtney Love phoned the Seattle police to report that Cobain was suicidal and that he'd locked himself in a room with a gun. When the police arrived, they discovered several guns as well as a bottle of pills, but Cobain claimed he wasn't suicidal—he said he'd locked himself in the room to get away from Love. A week later, Love arranged an intervention with several of Cobain's friends and concerned record company people. Reluctantly, Cobain agreed to go into rehab and flew down to LA to check in to the Exodus Recovery Center on March 30. The next day, he went outside to have a cigarette, and instead climbed over a six-foot fence, took a taxi to the LA Airport, and flew back to Seattle. He was seen around Seattle on April 2 and 3, but nobody seemed to know where he was staying. On April 3, Love hired an investigator to track him down. Five days later, an electrician hired to install security lighting around Cobain's house spotted a body on the floor of the apartment over the garage. Not seeing any signs of trauma, the electrician at first thought Cobain was asleep. Then he saw the gun.

Although conspiracy theorists of all stripes point an accusatory finger at various players in this tragedy, suggesting assorted murderous scenarios, the cause of death was originally stated as suicide by shotgun blast to the head, and nothing in the years of investigations, documentaries, blogs, websites, and other channels of paranoid innuendo since have changed that verdict.

In the sedate and leafy upper-middle class neighborhood of Madrona overlooking Lake Washington lies a small green space called **28 Viretta Park** (151 Lake Washington Blvd E.; www.seattle.gov/parks/park_detail.asp?ID=3098). The house where Kurt Cobain took his own life, most likely on April 5, 1994, is nearby. That date is considered by many to represent the symbolic end of the grunge era. A bench in Viretta Park has become an unofficial, informal shrine, where Cobain fans and admirers leave flowers and scrawl messages.

On April 10, 1994, thousands gathered around the fountain at the Flag Pavilion in the heart of the **29 Seattle Center** (305 Harrison Street; www.seattlecenter.com) to remember Kurt Cobain. People recall that everybody stood around slightly dazed, looking as if they were quietly, collectively, wondering "Why?" During the mostly sedate ceremony, Courtney Love read aloud parts of his suicide note, in which he complained about being a rock star. Then Love burst out, "Then why didn't you just fuckin' quit doing it, you asshole!" She got the crowd to shout out "Asshole" at Cobain in unison, an odd yet somehow fittingly warped tribute.

A somber moment in grunge history. A moment to step back and catch a breath, tour the Seattle Center, where the Cobain tribute took place. Pretend that death wasn't part of the grungy mix.

seattle center

Seattle Center occupies what was once open space to the north of downtown, in the shadow of Queen Anne Hill. The formerly meadowed area was transformed, beginning in the 1950s and culminating with the opening in April 1962 of the Seattle World's Fair, or Century 21 Exposition. This was a futuristic, optimistic event that drew 10 million people in six months, helped transform Seattle into a cosmopolitan port city, provided arenas for music and sports, and served as the location for one of Elvis Presley's many mediocre movies, this one called, cleverly, *It Happened at the World's Fair.*

Elvis aside, the center and its iconic Space Needle remain major elements in the Seattle civic self-image—a master plan generated in 2006 included a complete overhaul of the center, with a phase-out of the old-style carny amusement park areas and a major renovation of the stadium. The publicly funded overhaul is ongoing. The opera house has been remodeled into a world-class facility. On the pop music side, the Key Arena has been Seattle's large-scale concert arena of choice ever since opening. The creation of the center also led to the beginnings of Bumbershoot, Seattle's annual arts and music party, which features hundreds of bands, singers, poets, and performers of every possible type in a few dozen Seattle Center venues over Labor Day weekend in September.

From the grunge point of view, one of the most memorable Bumbershoot events took place way back in 1985, when that influential pre-grunge band the U-Men played at the Mural Amphitheater during Bumbershoot and lead singer John Bigley dropped a bottle of lighter fluid into the moat in front of the stage. He then lit a broom on fire and dropped it in the pool. Fire! The band played on, police attacked people in the audience, and center management soon filled in the moat. Grunge had announced its imminent arrival.

negativity takes hold

On the heels of Kurt Cobain's death, it seemed that the end of grunge was near. The death of Kristen Pfaff, the bassist in Courtney Love's band Hole, victim of a heroin overdose, on June 16 put another nail in grunge's coffin. She had planned to bail on Seattle and move to Minneapolis that very day.

It seemed that the trend in 1994 was people dying or becoming millionaire rock stars; the two were not always mutually exclusive. This was Seattle's new reality. These were American children, in their twenties, ill-equipped to deal with what the world threw at them, especially when heroin was added to the mix. Rock-and-roll god Jimi Hendrix, a Seattle boy, died back in the 1970s in his twenties of a drug overdose. There's a tradition here.

In 1995, the Seattle music community was still reeling from death and success dancing so closely together. Nirvana was gone, and Nirvana—whatever people thought of Kurt and Courtney and the band—represented grunge in the eyes of the world.

After what must have felt like endless touring to promote their assorted records, and having reached the very pinnacle of rock-and-roll mainstream success, Soundgarden drew back in 1995. They put their Grammy and MTV awards on the shelf, produced work in various alternative media, and did a short European tour in the fall. Their next studio album, *Down on the Upside*, was released in March 1996, and debuted at number two on the Billboard 200. The record marked a change in direction, with less heavy guitar work, lighter themes, and a less grungy sound. After the band toured with Metallica on the Lollapalooza main stage, a technical failure during the last show, in Hawaii on February 7, 1997, led to an onstage blow-up by bassist Ben Shepherd and a general retreat from the stage. In a precursor of what was to come, singer Chris Cornell reemerged on the stage and finished the set alone. The band quietly announced it was breaking up, more or less by mutual agreement, on April 9, 1997.

Chris Cornell went on with his career for a few years, doing a James Bond movie theme song, forming a new band called Audioslave with former members of Rage Against the Machine, and going solo. Ben Shepherd and Kim Thayil pursued various projects in the Seattle area. Drummer Matt Cameron joined Pearl Jam in 1998. Soundgarden reunited and began performing and recording again in 2010, and the band has since done several successful tours as well as released live concert material and recordings of new and old songs.

Early in 1995, Alice in Chains took some time off, and Layne Staley got involved with a "supergroup" of grunge players called Mad Season. With players from the Walkabouts, Pearl Jam, and Screaming Trees, Mad Season produced an album (Staley did lead vocals and album cover art) as well as a concert video shot live at Seattle's Moore Theatre.

In April of that year, Alice in Chains went back into the studio— into the **㉚ Bad Animals Studio** (2212 4th Avenue, www.badanimals. com) in Seattle, owned by the Wilson sisters of Heart—to record a new album. Eponymously named *Alice in Chains*, the record was released on November 7, 1995, immediately landed in the number one spot on the Billboard 200 chart, and eventually was certified double platinum. When the band did not tour in support of the album, new rumors of drug abuse by Staley began making the rounds.

On April 10, 1996, the band emerged from their hiatus to perform a live concert for *MTV Unplugged*. They played several of their hits and one new song, and released an album of the show a few months later. It debuted at number three on the Billboard 200 chart.

Staley became even more of a recluse after the death of his fiancé in 1996. In the years that followed, he seldom performed or even appeared, although he did record music with the band, which put out half a dozen more albums, including early material, live show recordings, rarities, outtakes, and greatest hits compilations.

Layne Staley was found dead of a heroin and crack overdose on April 9, 2002. He had been dead about two weeks, which says a lot about how isolated he had become. Eight years after the Kurt Cobain tribute in 1994, a similar candlelight tribute was held at the same location, Seattle Center's Flag Pavilion, for Layne Staley, lead singer of Alice in Chains.

"It's better to burn out / Than to fade away," sang Neil Young back in 1979. It was hard to tell which of those things grunge was doing by 2002, but it was definitely heading for the exit. If grunge had been an era, that era was over.

the documentaries: hype! and montage of heck

A couple of nonfiction films—one early, one late—capture the grunge era in all its gore and glory.

Hype! was shot between 1992 and 1994 (with plenty of earlier archival footage) and released in 1996 after winning the Grand Jury Prize at the Sundance Film Festival the previous January. *Hype!* was directed by Doug Pray, a film maker from California who was coaxed by producer Steve Helvey (the film was coproduced by Pete Vogt and Lisa Dutton) into coming north to Seattle to document the grunge scene.

"This is really an amazing story," Pray said in an interview. "You have a small handful of bands—about twenty people who in the course of five or six years completely changed pop culture. They . . . totally revolutionized the music industry. I mean, Nirvana singlehandedly did, but all those bands were part of that."

What these musicians were part of, and what this movie assiduously and amusingly documents, is a startling collision of a native-grown artistic movement—in the form of rock-and-roll—and commercialism —in the form of record companies, fashion designers, department stores, and every manner of money-hungry corporate leech. That weird collision, and the Seattle music community's response to it, shapes the movie's narrative as it traces the scene from the mid-1980s for about ten years, to when several bands hit the big time in the early to mid-1990s.

"Actually, nobody really knows what grunge was," Pray said. "If you look at it as a group of bands or as a community of people who didn't take themselves seriously and played pretty loud, fun music—and even the dark, heavy stuff is kind of fun—then yeah, [that's grunge]. I don't know even so much if there's a sound than there is an attitude that everybody shared."

Part of that attitude was resistance to hype—the push to commercialize, exploit, or even take seriously "the scene." This resistance was exemplified by Sub Pop employee Megan Jasper's fake glossary of grunge that made its way into the *New York Times*. Jasper gives her take on how that farce happened, while both Sub Pop impresarios—Bruce Pavitt and Jonathan Poneman—offer their interpretations of the scene, or scam, or hustle, that was grunge. Sub Pop's role as a major source of the hype, through its cultivation of British journalist Everett True and other promotional means, is implicit in the story, of course. After all, hyping the scene and making fun of the hype at the same time were part of the deal. The Sub Pop guys had their cake, they ate it too, and then they threw it in everybody's faces.

The commercialization of the music proved irresistible: no matter how righteously egalitarian they might be, grunge band members were performers, and few rock-and-roll musicians would turn down a chance to tour the world, become rich and famous, and be fawned over by the media and adored by fans. Yet right through the whole grunge era, while some bands were riding the commercialization train, plenty of other Seattle musicians insisted that it was all a big joke and they didn't give a fuck. These stalwart souls are finely displayed in the movie, laughing at themselves, their suddenly rich and famous friends, the hustle going on all around them. There is some understandable bitterness, for some of these guys are maybe a little pissed that it was Soundgarden and not their band that became famous. There is some sadness as well, quietly and respectfully implicit in the extended footage of a live nightclub performance by the Gits, whose lead singer Mia Zapata was brutally murdered in 1993.

Although released in 1996, when grunge was no means D.O.A., *Hype!* prefigures grunge's death by overdose of success. As well as featuring many live nightclub performances (including some great grainy amateur footage of Nirvana doing its first live performance of "Smells Like Teen Spirit"), the movie also has arena concert footage of Soundgarden. Early on, in the clubs, the audiences and the bands are in it together, for that's what grunge was about. When we watch the audience arriving at the arena for the after-they-hit-the-big-time Soundgarden show, we see them passing through security checks, walking down concrete stairwells and passageways, entering a huge, dark, dehumanized arena—although it is still rock-and-roll and Soundgarden puts on a good show, this is a totally different experience. It's been paved and is not at all grungy. As John Lennon sang, long before grunge, "the dream is over."

Some twenty years later, another movie offered an even grimmer view, suggesting that if it had been a dream, it had been a very *bad* dream, at least for grunge's most famous representative. *Kurt Cobain: Montage of Heck* was released in 2015, having taken eight years to put together. Directed by Brett Morgen, the documentary is a revelation, not for any specific gossip or particular sordid revelations—everybody pretty much knew how fucked up Cobain was—but simply because it reveals Cobain for the complex, enigmatic, and, well, tortured, man—and artist—he really was. The movie makes it clear that Kurt was not under Courtney's thumb, not at all. They lived a mad life, squalid, fun, and miserable. Kurt was a deeply unhappy, hypersensitive soul; this is made clear in the film. A lot of the visual imagery is based on Cobain's cartoons, drawings, and writings—and much of it is disturbing if not downright frightening.

The movie also shows that Love and Cobain were junkies. Love claims to have quit while she was pregnant, and, given how healthy Frances appears to be in the movie, the story seems believable. But Cobain, who nods his way through several scenes, evidently hadn't quit. That will come as no surprise to anyone on the scene back in the day. In some respects, heroin ruled his life.

Courtney Love comes off all right in the film considering her reputation as Cobain's Black Widow. According to the *New York Times*, it was Love who originally approached the director Morgen about doing the film, agreeing that she would have no control over the final cut. Many of us in Seattle at the time put all the blame for Cobain's suicide on Courtney Love, but the movie seems to say otherwise: it wasn't about her or their relationship. Cobain was a wretchedly unhappy soul, a man incapable of dealing with his life, and so he chose to end it. With his suicide, he ended the most intense and deranged moment in the short history of grunge.

by the way #6

other movies inspired by kurt cobain

Kurt Cobain, dead by suicide in 1994 at the unripe young age of twenty-seven (Jimi Hendrix, Jim Morrison of the Doors, and Janis Joplin all died at twenty-seven), inspired several film makers to explore the tragic story of his life and death. Films about Cobain include Gus Van Sant's *Last Days*; the documentary *About a Son* (directed by A. J. Schnack and coproduced by Michael Azerrad, who wrote a book about Cobain and Nirvana); and *Kurt and Courtney*, Nick Broomfield's documentary on the circumstances of Cobain's death and what his wife may or may not have had to do with it.

The best and most informative of the three is *About a Son*, a kind of autobiographical meditation on Kurt Cobain—autobiographical in that the entire movie features Cobain speaking in his own voice, from taped interviews made by writer Michael Azerrad, about his childhood and adolescence, his musical path, and the effects of almost overnight fame and celebrity. It does not trade in tabloid trash but instead, with images taken from the Pacific Northwest places that shaped Cobain's life, paints a personal portrait of the artist as a young man.

Van Sant's nominally fictional *Last Days* features a famous rock star musician at the end of his rope, the end of his life, a drug-addicted young man in a haze, unable to relate to anyone or anything. He wanders around his enormous house, spends much of his time alone, and eventually dies. While a disclaimer says the film's characters are "in part, fictional," the film is dedicated to Kurt Cobain.

With a title inspired by another film about a drug-addicted rock star and his crazy wife (*Sid and Nancy*), *Kurt and Courtney* documents director Nick Broomfield's attempt to investigate the conspiracy theories surrounding the death of Kurt Cobain. There were (and are) many people certain that Courtney Love had Cobain murdered; chief among these conspiracy theorists is Love's own father, Hank Harrison, who wrote two books about it. The movie evolves into an indictment of Love for her unwillingness to appear in the film and for her later attempts at suppressing it. Although inconclusive, it does have some weirdly compelling moments, and for those not in love with Ms. Love, perhaps it makes its case.

Pearl Jam's Eddie Vedder in Rome, Italy, when the band toured with U2 in 1993.

chapter 7

roll away the stone

Grunge as a musical moment and movement belongs in the history books, but quite a few of its pioneers are still playing on, some of them strapping on their old guitars and playing the same four chords they played back in the early 1990s, others out there learning new ones or blazing entirely new trails.

The guys Kurt left behind in Nirvana have turned out to be amazingly creative and productive. Between work with his own band—the entertaining rock-and-roll band the Foo Fighters—side projects of all kinds, and raising a family, Nirvana's last and best drummer has had huge success. He's even done a TV series, *Sonic Highways*, in which he explored America's musical history and roots and played with great musicians all over the country. On stage, video, or TV, Dave Grohl seems to be having a hell of a good time, rocking and rolling his way through life.

Krist Novoselic, Nirvana's long-time bass player and friend of Kurt Cobain from Aberdeen, has had a slightly less illustrious career, musically speaking, in the post-Nirvana years. He has been in several different bands with different lineups, none quite sticking. From 2006 to 2010, he joined the long-time punk band Flipper; in 2011, he played on the Foo Fighters' album *Wasting Light*.

However, Novoselic can claim a considerable number of accomplishments as a political activist. In the Nirvana years, he was involved in fighting assorted laws designed to censor or suppress rock-and-roll and other forms of musical expression that challenged the powers of the state. In the years since, he has proven to be a serious political activist, lobbyist, and generally low-key but effective gadfly speaking out on behalf of young people, musicians, the disenfranchised, and all manner of oppressed citizens. He has even published a book on the topic, *Of Grunge and Government: Let's Fix this Broken Democracy*. Novoselic DJs a radio show out of Astoria, Oregon, and writes a political blog for the *Seattle Weekly Online*.

One can only wonder what a smart puppy like Kurt Cobain might have accomplished, with or without Nirvana, had he managed to get through those tortured years of youth and grown into a mature artist. It's interesting to see that his daughter, Frances Bean Cobain, is making a name for herself as a visual artist in New York. Her mother, Courtney Love, is still a celebrity of a certain kind these days, and she wears that mantle well enough. In 2015, for instance, she made a guest-starring appearance as a rock-and-roll singer pretty much based on herself on the hit TV series *Empire*.

pearl jams on

There is no better example of how the music of tortured youth can evolve into intelligent, mature rock-and-roll artistry, with plenty of sympathy for the next generation, than that set by the members of Pearl Jam, both as individuals and as a band. Ever since they attempted in Don Quixote-like fashion, back in 1993–94, to take on the monopolist Ticketmaster—in an effort to keep ticket prices for their concerts down—Pearl Jam as a band and its individual members have consistently used their fame and influence to promote countless politically progressive and green issues and to raise money for disaster relief, progressive political candidates, schools, nongovernmental organizations, and institutions devoted to humanitarian and ecological causes.

They have accomplished all this while recording and releasing one million-selling album after another to the general public; releasing dozens of special singles and albums to their devoted fans; and engaging in numerous national and international tours to support the music. Each of the members of Pearl Jam has worked in all sorts of unusual and intriguing musical side projects.

In 2011, Cameron Crowe made a movie called *Pearl Jam Twenty*. It's a revealing documentary about the Seattle music scene, more even-handed and positive than either *Hype!* or *Montage of Heck* even if you aren't a devotee of all things Pearl Jam. Along with celebrating what Pearl Jam accomplished in their first twenty years as a band, the movie explores their struggles with fame and fortune, the Danish concert tragedy that left nine fans dead, and their legal battles with Ticketmaster (and other powers that be) through archival footage and interviews, and it is simply great material. Crowe has been a part of the rock-and-roll world since he started writing for *Rolling Stone* when he was fifteen, and is an accomplished filmmaker as well (*Singles*, with its grungy Seattle settings and cameos from soon-to-be grunge stars, only gets better with time). He is tight with the band, and it's obvious. They let him into their world.

One other thing you take away from watching *Pearl Jam Twenty* is the steadfast devotion of Pearl Jam's large, international fan base. Listening to the fans interviewed in the movie brought to mind one other band that had a similarly committed army of followers: the Grateful Dead and their Deadheads. In both instances, the band and its followers formed a community.

For more than two decades, Pearl Jam has set an example of rock-and-roll soul and integrity. The guys in Pearl Jam—Eddie Vedder, Stone Gossard, Mike McCready, Jeff Ament, and Matt Cameron—have turned grunge into good and into gold, and they've done it while generously and consistently giving back to the community and the world.

reunions

Several other grungy luminaries are also still making themselves heard, at least from time to time.

In 2005, Alice in Chains reunited for a benefit concert with a new singer. Subsequently, the band reformed with William Duvall as the lead singer. Alice in Chains has since been touring on and off, and released *Black Gives Way to Blue* in September 2009. The album features a guest appearance by Elton John on the title track, a tribute to Layne Staley. *The Devil Put Dinosaurs Here*, followed in 2013, and yet another is said to be in the works.

Soundgarden, which disbanded in 1997 amid internal tensions, reunited a dozen years later, in 2010, and were one of the headliners at Lollapalooza that year. They put out an album of new music, *King Animal*, in 2012; a compilation of live tracks and rarities, *Echo of Miles*, in 2014; and were said to be working on another new album in early 2016.

One band that's definitely keeping alive the original spirit of grunge is Mudhoney, still playing together after all these years and still writing new songs and performing them live along with all the old semi-hits. They released a new record in 2015, did a tour, and have a new band biography coming out soon. Like the other bands, they have their websites, one old, one new, with all the usual bells and whistles, including biographies of the band members that further reveal the early roots of grunge in Seattle.

While much of the new music from these bands sounds much like the original music (perhaps more sophisticated in terms of production), the lyrics are definitely offering a different point of view. These are not angst-ridden adolescents or twenty-somethings anymore, and their new songs reflect that.

It's easy to cast a cynical eye on these reunions of mostly well-to-do middle-age men, and say, "They're in it for the money." And maybe there's some truth in it—but what's wrong with doing it for the money, at least in part? People grow accustomed to their creature comforts.

More to the point, don't they deserve the chance to rekindle for their fans the fire they started? These songwriters had insightful things to say about anguished youth in all its myriad Seattle variations in their day, and they earned the right to say it again. They originally formed these bands because they were like-minded, musically or philosophically (or however you articulate what it is that makes certain people play music together well). So, why not get together and start playing again? Whatever pissed them off or broke up the bands back in the day is in the past now.

Maybe the stakes aren't quite as high, existentially speaking, but these guys are serious rock-and-roll musicians and singers and often-inspired songwriters; being professional performers, they want to play for an audience. Maybe it isn't down and dirty grunge anymore—it's hard to thrash around on the floor and stage dive into the audience when you're over forty—but that doesn't make it illegitimate.

here we are now, entertain us

Seattle today is a far cry from the city it was twenty-five years ago, when it was a murky, semibroke corner of the forgotten Pacific northwest, nurturing a golden future as a high-tech hub of the world. That golden future arrived with a vengeance, and neighborhoods formerly associated with the low-rent life of grunge are today besieged with high-rise construction both residential and commercial. Times have certainly changed. Seattle's football team is one of the best in the country! And yet . . . Seattle still has a place for the quirky, the offbeat, and yes, the grungy.

In Seattle, Sub Pop continues to thrive as a midsize record label, with numerous bands hitting it big nationally and internationally. Some Sub Pop bands sound grungy, others are wildly different. The Afghan Whigs, Band of Horses, the Murder City Devils, Flight of the Conchords, and Fleet Foxes—just a handful of the many successful artists on the Sub Pop label—play radically different styles of music, ranging from hard, grungy rock-and-roll to celestially harmonic folk rock. Sub Pop might have started with grunge, but it has a lot more to offer these days.

One might say the same thing about the city of Seattle as a music town. Looking back now, what we see is that grunge came out of a music scene in Seattle that was unique: the guys in the bands were friends, and rather than being competitive (like the musicians in LA and New York, for example, as Crowe points out in *Pearl Jam Twenty*), they looked out for each other and took pride in what the others did as well as in what they did themselves. Although there were a lot of angry young men and plenty of mind- and body-altering or -abusing substances on the scene, that scene was also nurturing and mutually supportive. It echoes the paradox of rock-and-roll: fundamentally angry music intended to bring on ecstasy.

When exactly the grunge moment passed doesn't matter. Seattle evolved into a rock-and-roll city with energy to spare, and remains one today. The scene has had its ups and downs over the past few decades— heroin didn't help—but the bands still play on. Seattle is booming and so is the city's musical scene.

For readers wanting to pay the city a visit and perhaps check in with a few of the iconic grunge spots, you can use this book as a road map. But don't ignore what's going on today. Several dozen clubs and theaters offer live music in Seattle, including old standbys the Showbox, the Moore, Jazz Alley, Neumo's, Tula's, the Central Saloon, and the one and only Crocodile Café. These venues and a couple of others, including the Triple Door and the Paramount, are downtown or close to it on Capitol Hill, in (perpetually skanky) Belltown, or in the increasingly gentrified Pioneer Square. If you venture farther afield, you'll find the Skychurch stage at the EMP at Seattle Center, along with the all-ages Vera Project. In the shadow of the I-5 freeway, El Corazon rocks posh South Lake Union. Formerly eccentric and ignored but now-trendy Ballard is home to thousands of apartments in entire blocks of new buildings, half-a-dozen "hot" restaurants, and some great live music venues, including the Sunset Tavern and the Tractor. Ballard might be trendy, but the taverns are old school—grungy, you might say. Up

Leary Way from Ballard, in Fremont, you'll find the High Dive and the Nectar Lounge; way out in Greenlake, the Little Red Hen is Seattle's main country music venue.

There are a dozen other joints and theaters offering live shows two, four, and even seven nights a week. Check the local listings when you get to town. Seattle is a lively and much-visited destination city these days, and it keeps growing bigger, faster, and more popular. Everywhere you, you hear voices speaking foreign languages. Voices that belong not only to the geniuses imported to invent new devices and Internet- and cloud-based ways to use them, but also to tourists! Tourists from other countries are putting Seattle on their itineraries. How about that? Why not? It's a beautiful city, especially in summer, and there is plenty to do here.

Taking the grunge tour is one great way to discover Seattle. Like the city itself, the music scene that grunge jumpstarted twenty-five years ago continues to grow in size and sophistication. The twenty-first just might be Seattle's century.

notes

chapter 1

4: "Because of this…": "Artist of the Year: Nirvana," *Spin*, December 1992.

8: "Or was it a joke…": from *Hype!*, directed by Doug Pray, produced by Doug Helvey, Lisa Dutton, Pete Vogt (1995).

13: "The jazz scene played a role…": Quincy Jones quote is from Paul de Barros, *Jackson Street After Hours: The Roots of Jazz in Seattle* (Seattle: Sasquatch, 1993).

chapter 2

21: "According to Clark Humphrey…": Clark Humphrey, *Loser: The Real Seattle Music Story* (New York: Harry N. Abrams, 1999), 63.

22: "The geographical inspiration behind…": Poneman quote is from Martin Aston, "Freak Scene," in *Q: Nirvana and the Story of Grunge* (December 2005), 12; Arm quote is from Mick Wall, "Northwest Passage," in *Q: Nirvana and the Story of Grunge* (December 2005), 9; Chris Hanzsek quote is from an interview with the author, 2008.

23: "What you had were a bunch…": Author interview with Charles Peterson, 2008; Endino quote is from *Hype!*

23: "Then there was money…": Author interview with Art Chantry, 2008.

24: "Finally, there is attitude…": Author conversation with Lisa Dutton, 2008.

25: "I feel stupid…": Written by Kurt Cobain, Krist Novoselic, and Dave Grohl, "Smells Like Teen Spirit" was released on Nirvana's album *Nevermind* (DGC Records, 1991).

25: "Touch me I'm sick…": Written by Mark Arm, Steve Turner, Dan Peters, and Matt Lukin, "Touch Me I'm Sick" was released as a single by Sub Pop in 1988.

26: "For all that…": Author interview with Susan Silver, 2008.

27: "A joint called…": Author interview with Art Chantry, 2008.

29: "When Soundgarden first started…": Author conversation with Lisa Dutton, 2008.

31: "When grunge got big…": Interview with Mark Arm by Douglas Wolk, posted July 10, 2008, on *Pitchfork*, http://pitchfork.com/features/interviews/7147-mark-arm/.

33: "In June 1986…": Michael Azerrad, *Our Band Could Be Your Life: Scenes from the American Indie Underground, 1981–1991* (Boston: Little, Brown, 2001).

34: "It is important to note…": Azerrad, *Our Band Could Be Your Life*.

35: "Chantry moved to Seattle…": Author interview with Art Chantry, 2008.

chapter 3

39: "Toward the end of 1987…": From a *Rolling Stone* podcast posted online, June 16, 2006, interview with Jeff Ament by managing editor Will Dana.

40: "Layne Staley was born…": Adriana Rubio and Layne Staley, *Layne Staley, Angry Chair: A Look Inside the Heart & Soul of an Incredible Musician* (Evansdale, IA: Xanadu, 2003).

41: "Gloria sent me pictures…": Written by Jerry Cantrell, the single "Rooster" was included on Alice in Chains' album *Dirt* (Columbia Records, 1993).

42: "You might say…": Definitions come from the *Britannica Concise Encyclopedia* online; Cobain quote is from Michael Azerrad, *Come as You Are: The Story of Nirvana* (New York: Doubleday, 1994), 62.

43: "Through Jack Endino's contacts…": From *Hype!*

46: "A few months later…": nterview with Mark Arm by Douglas Wolk, posted July 10, 2008, on *Pitchfork*, http://pitchfork.com/features/interviews/7147-mark-arm/.

48: "All my friends are brown…": Written by Chris Cornell in 1992 for the soundtrack of the movie *Singles* (an acoustic version is part of the background soundtrack), "Spoonman" was released on Soungarden's album *Superunknown* (A&M Records, 1994).

51: "Pearl Jam's Mike McCready…": Gillian G. Garr, "If These Walls Could Rock," *Seattle Times Online*, March 6, 2005.

chapter 4

56: "True went on…": From Everett True, *Nirvana: The Biography* (New York: Da Capo, 2007).

56: "One of the main events…": Azerrad, *Come As You Are.*

59: "Get me to the stage…": Written by Andrew Wood, Jeff Ament, Bruce Fairweather, Greg Gilmore, and Stone Gossard, "This is Shangrila" was released on Mother Love Bone's album *Apple* (Stardog/Mercury Records, 1990).

61: "I'm the man in the box…": Written by Jerry Cantrell and Layne Staley, "I'm the Man in the Box" was released on Alice in Chains' album *Facelift* (Columbia Records, 1990).

61: "As Jerry Cantrell once said…": Jon Wiederhorn, "To Hell and Back," in *Rolling Stone* (February 1996).

63: "Backstreet lover…": Written by Stone Gossard and Eddie Vedder, "Once" was released on Pearl Jam's album *Ten* (Epic Records, 1991).

chapter 5

76: "Long-time *Rolling Stone* writer…": Cameron Crowe, "A Film Maker's Diary," *Rolling Stone* (October 1992).

81: "Things took a negative turn…": *Melody Maker*, June 20, 1992.

82: "Sargent's death represented…": Thomas Frank, "Harsh Realm, Mr. Sulzberger!" in *The Baffler* (Winter/Spring 1993).

83: "Teenage angst has paid off well…": Written by Kurt Cobain, "Serve the Servants" was released on Nirvana's album *In Utero* (DGC Records, 1993).

chapter 6

95: "On January 25, 1994…": Paul Evans in *Rolling Stone*, review posted online, http://www.rollingstone.com/artists/aliceinchains/albums/album/284284/review/6211567/jar_of_flies.

97: "On April 10, 1994…": Steven Hill, "Who Will Tell Generation X? A Eulogy for Nirvana's Kurt Cobain, 1967–1994," published in the *New Internationalist and Washington Free Press*, http://www.giantleap.org/envision/cobain.htm.

101: "This is really an amazing story...": Rich Drees, "A Decade after the Hype! An Archival Interview with Director Doug Pray," www.filmbuffonline.com/Features/Hype/DougPray%27sHype.htm.

102: "Actually, nobody really knows...": Drees, "A Decade after the Hype."

credits

Cover: (top) iStock.com/Aguru; (bottom) iStock.com/raelro

Page 2: © Josef Scaylea / CORBIS

Page 18: © Charles Peterson / Retna Ltd. / Corbis

Page 38: © Sub Pop

Page 54: All images © Donna Day

Page 67: Courtesy Chris Hanzsek

Page 68: © Lance Mercer

Page 93: © Lance Mercer

Page 94: (top) © Lance Mercer

Page 94: (bottom) © John Van Hasselt / Sygma / Corbis

Page 108: © Lance Mercer

Page 133: © Donna Day

index

about the author

Justin Henderson is the author of several books on architecture and interior design and has coauthored or edited multiple guidebooks. He is also the author of several mystery novels. After living in New York City from 1978 to 1991, Justin moved to Seattle, where he experienced the grunge scene firsthand. In 2009, he relocated with his family to Sayulita, Mexico, where he did a lot of surfing and writing before returning to a far-less-grungy Seattle in 2014. He passed away in 2017.